Let's Talk About Adoption

– JACQUELINE HEARN MBE –

An environmentally friendly book printed and bound in England by
www.printondemand-worldwide.com

FastPrint Publishing

www.fast-print.net/store.php

LET'S TALK ABOUT ADOPTION
Copyright © Jacqueline Hearn MBE 2014

A catalogue record for this book is available from the British Library

ISBN 978-178456-050-8

.

First published 2014 by
FASTPRINT PUBLISHING
Peterborough, England.

My Thanks

Jason and Sarah for their persistence and assistance without them this book would never have got started and for supporting me so well.

Deborah Blake for her patience, understanding excellent proofreading.

My wonderful husband Roger without his recall and humour I could never have got here.

With Love, and many thanks to our Adopters and Friends for their contributions.

With respect and admiration for all Adopters and Foster Carers everywhere.

For all the Social Workers at Cambridge Social Service for the help and assistance I was given to write this book, especially John Abankwa, social worker and friend

Nigel Barrett (www.nigelphoto.com/) for his flair and generosity

Thanks to the design team at Fast-Print Publishing

To Jackie
Best Wishes
Jacqueline
x

To

Roger

xxx

Contents

LET'S TALK ABOUT ADOPTION

1. Biography

Jacqueline Hearn was born in south-east London in 1947. Her parents had their own business and she grew up with her younger sister in an active business environment.

She attended State schools and was not particularly academic save for her love of mathematics. Jacqueline left school at the age of 15 and joined the family business. She met her husband to be in 1962 and they married in 1965. Their first child, a daughter, was born in 1967.

It was whilst caring for her first child that Jacqueline saw an advertisement in the local paper for the Local Authority: "Foster Carers Wanted". She applied and was accepted and within six months Jacqueline had her first pre-adoption baby.

This was the start of a career as a Local Authority foster career spanning 44 years. She went on to have two more children of her own and adopt a further three children as well as to foster goodness knows how many others.

The children she fostered were predominantly 0 to 11 years but also included teenagers, and some unmarried mothers and their babies. But overall her specialty was fostering babies and toddlers, which included relinquished babies and children who were going for adoption.

Nobody knows exactly how many infants Jacqueline fostered because in the early days she was shared between various London boroughs. At one time Jacqueline had her own family group home under the guidance of Tower Hamlets where she predominately took two family group placements of three to four children each. These placements were for days or sometimes months.

In 1996 Jacqueline retired from fostering for a while because her own children were reaching adolescence. Jacqueline was awarded an MBE for her services to young people in 1994.

However, a few years later she returned as a foster carer with Cambridge County Council where she continued to care for babies and young children until finally retiring in June 2013.

2. Why a Book?

There are a lot of pressures put on prospective adopters as to the rights and wrongs of raising babies and young children.

By writing my experiences down I hope to alleviate some of the stress placed upon prospective adopters. My writings are predominantly for guidance and are not intended as a bible or as something that must be done. It is a chance to read, discuss and then formulate your own practices.

I am going to explain the process of actually adopting a baby or child and the handover procedure. I will then relate some of my experiences involving the adoption of babies through to 10-year-olds, followed by some of the experiences I gained with young children in the seventies and eighties, and how these helped me form my practices. Then I will conclude with observations from some of the adopters I have come to know and respect over the years.

The babies and children who have passed through my care have gone to loving parents from all walks of life. Adoptive parents only get a period of a few months' notice that they are going to receive a placement. It has been my task to give them the guidance and confidence to receive their charge as well as prepare the child for moving on.

As a prospective adopter there will be many hurdles to jump, but once you are there you will be able to enjoy one of the greatest pleasures we can experience and if my notes can help ease your mind then I will have achieved what I set out to do.

For those contemplating adoption I hope my book will be enough to encourage you to take the first steps. However if, after reading this book, you feel adoption is not for you then I hope to give you some inspiration to become a Local Authority foster carer. One thing is certain the children need you and a secure home, which you can give them.

3. Why Adopt?

This is what my parents asked me when I told them that we were going to adopt the three children we had been fostering for some time. Our reply was "because we want to, and because we can. These children need a permanent home in which they can thrive, develop and be loved". There were lots of "what ifs", but we felt the children's needs and our ability to provide them far outweighed any "what ifs". As far as our own children were concerned the three foster children had been with us for so long that they were already an integral part our family.

Modern day adoption allows people from all walks of life to adopt a child, whether you are married, single, gay or disabled, does not prevent you from adopting a child. As long as you can prove that you can provide a room in a loving home, and an environment that can give a child the chance to grow and reach their potential, then you can apply to adopt.

As we get older we will all reflect on what we have done in our life. What a great achievement is open to so many people, to give a home and share the life of a child. A young person, who at the time of your intervention had little or no prospect of having a permanent home to call their own, or a place where they could be part of a functioning family.

By making enquiries at your Local Authority Adoption Department you will find out where you may be able to fit in. There are so many children of all ages needing an adoptive home of their very own. You should not let your age deter you from applying. Whilst you may not fit the criteria for having a baby, you may well be an ideal placement for a five to six-year-old. In some cases middle age could be a positive advantage. Parents who have had children who have grown and flown the nest have the benefit of experience, and this can be so important in helping to give the children a warm, understanding and loving home. A lot of children who have been born to very young parents can often settle with more mature adopters, because a child relates age to security. I can personally vouch for this with recent foster placements that have been in my care. Another misconception is that adopters have to be wealthy; this is not so. You do have to prove that you are financially stable and have a suitable income to provide for a child. There is no initial commitment required and you will be guided all the way. Not every adoption works, children are very complex with special needs, but to take that journey with them and to help them fulfil their potential is a fantastic experience.

On the television we see charity appeals for children in other countries that need help and, quite rightly, we send cash and have fund raising events. However there are a so many children right under our noses in desperate need of a place to belong, but they seem to get no publicity at all. When they do it is most probably as a result of a tragedy being reported in the media. The problem is that for every one case reported;

many more that are not. Children needing care and protection do not make good political headlines and there is a tendency to focus on one scapegoat in these cases and then brush it all away. Ideally we would have a never ending army of support workers with which we could stop these incidents taking place, but the truth is we do not and never will have. Even if we did there would still be the one case that would slip through the net or go undetected. A brave head of Social Services recently said that he was confident that he had the correct strategies and support packages in place to protect the children in his borough. The problem was that he had never had more that 75% of the required staffing level needed to supply those necessary services.

By adopting we can hope to change the future. By providing a warm and caring environment we will install in the child the notional seed, so that when they become adults they will want to provide the same loving home for their own children.

The other day I heard about a couple who met and married in their late 30s. They are conservationists and believe there are many children in this country that need a home. They are forgoing the risk of trying to have children at their age and are preparing to apply to adopt straightaway. They want to help the population and not add to it. I find this to be a level of commitment rarely found.

4. A Little Bit of History

I started being a foster carer in 1968 and back then I was known as a foster mother. I have lost count of how many babies and children have passed through my care. I have seen many practices and procedures come full circle and start back round again.

As a foster carer the practice of keeping in contact with the child and the adopter is now being encouraged if only as a distant relative. This practice has only been developed and encouraged over the last four or five years, before this time once the child had left my care further contact was discouraged. If we go further back to the 60s and 70s it was forbidden. The current practice is based on the fact that it is not good for a child to live with you and then suddenly, to all intents and purposes, have you disappear. It is believed that the ongoing effect on the child could mean that they mistrust future relationships on the basis that they too may just disappear. Finding the right amount of contact, and what form it should take is still under review.

In pursuing the current practice adopters have informed me that the methods I use for the introduction of the child to them, the handover procedure and the follow-on guidance that I have offered is by no means universal. It is at their request that I have written this book to help guide future adopters through what to expect at the practical end of things.

I will also try to give you some tips and pointers on what to expect from a child's behaviour towards you in the early days. Finally I will relate some of the experiences of having children in my care from several years ago, and the little lessons that they have taught me in developing my practice at the time. However I hope my book stimulates you to make your own choices as to the practices you will use when you adopt.

It is not my intention to comment on anything to do with the adoption process with which I have not had personal experience. So if I do not mention private adoption and fostering agencies it is not because of anything detrimental to them. It is purely that I have not worked in their sphere.

In the late 1960s

When I started fostering, children who were to be adopted came from two main sources. Either they came by way of tragically losing one or both parents or because their mother was unmarried. Unmarried motherhood was stigmatised and life was made quite unbearable for the mother, so much so that they felt they had no other option than to have their child adopted. The newborn babies only stayed with me for about six weeks or until the birth mum had signed the adoption papers. Once that had happened a social worker collected baby from me and then went on to hand baby to the new adoptive family. I never met the adopters or knew where baby went.

When parents were in situations which meant that they were unable to care for their children and it was felt that the children were not safe, they were placed into the care of the Local Authority and thus into foster care. Most of the children came into care on a voluntary basis usually as a result of a family crisis. If it were felt this placement would only be temporary then the child would be placed with a short-term foster carer.

These short-term foster carers usually had placements for anything up to six months. If the situation was more long term then the child would be placed with long-term foster carers who would be prepared to care for the child on a permanent basis until they were 18. This arrangement suited the foster care availability quite well as there were carers who were happy to care for a child in the short term, but were not able to make the long-term commitment. By the same token there were foster carers who wished to make a more long term commitment and many of the children were to remain in care till they were 18 or even 21. One thing to note with foster caring in those times was that the difference between short and long-term caring had very clearly defined barriers, you were either one or the other.

There were inherent problems in this system, particularly because circumstances were prone to change. What at first appeared to be short term ended up being long term and vice versa and this would mean that the child would have to be moved from one carer to another, and this was obviously very disruptive for the child. In current practice we still have short term and long term careers, but short term now is for up to three years and long term can be up to 18 to 21 years or when the child is ready to move on.

The 70s and 80s

With the onset of drug dependency and rising alcohol abuse, the amount of children coming into care steadily began to rise, outstripping the number of available foster carers and the Local Authority budgets as well. Tremendous pressure was also placed on Social Services staffing levels, pressures that exist today.

At the same time, we became a member of the EU and subject to their legislation in social care. It was not long before new regulations were brought into effect, which in very simple terms stated that the rights, interests and welfare of the child became paramount. Therefore what was best for the child took precedent over the wishes of the parent. In line with this legislation it was felt that a child coming into care with little or no hope of being able to go home in the future was not being best served by staying in long-term care. The security of adoption was a far better option to meet the child's long-term needs. Those that fostered became known as foster carers and not foster mothers.

Over a period of around 35 years we have gone from mainly babies requiring adoption, to having children of all ages that fit the bill.

The whole point of adoption is to provide a loving and stable home where a child of any age can thrive and develop to the best of their abilities.

Present day

There are very few babies presented for adoption and even fewer white babies. Despite their young age some of these children, because of their past, may have developmental issues and in some cases health issues. Their very situation also makes attachment difficulties a real possibility. I have known people contemplating adoption to shy away from these facts, and yet children born into a functioning relationship can also develop these issues, it is part of life. A loving home can improve the wellbeing of these children and in some cases can reverse the impact of their previous life.

There are no guarantees in anything. What you can be sure of is that as an adopter, you will be fully briefed and no pressures are brought to bear on your final decision to proceed. You will also have support networks on hand to help guide you through. There is tremendous satisfaction from negotiating these matters and seeing your adopted child develop into a happy and fulfilled young adult.

Communication

All adopted children need to know about their birth family and why they ended up being adopted. They need this to be able to rationalise and to make sense of it all. This will become particularly important when they approach and enter adolescence. It is equally important that you are prepared to embrace this open approach and assist as much as it is required. It would be devastating if adopters do not keep up this open approach and try to hide the adoption. Sooner or later it will all come out and the revelation will present so many problems, including the child's trust in you. If you have kept this from them then it would stand to reason that they would wonder what else you have kept from them. There are so many stories of the hurt and damage caused to the adopted child by not being informed until late into their life. The truth gently put in an age appropriate way is the only path to take. Let's face it with the communication technology that is available today it is not hard for children to find out anything they wish to. Better to stay with them than to force them into secrecy.

I have worked in both eras of practice. The say nothing, keep it quiet and pretend it has never happened era and the current open and honest approach. I can assure you that whilst it may take more input from the adopter, the current approach is best and pays more dividends in the long run.

It is not my job, nor should it become yours, to justify whether a child should be adopted or not. Ours is to serve the needs of the child and trust in the decision of a court.

I cannot comment on the process for selecting suitable adopters other than to say that you should approach your Local Authority or adoption agency, and they in turn will send a social worker to interview you and the ball rolls on from there. They will have to make enquiries, seek references and check that you have the necessary room. This will culminate in your application going before a Local Authority Panel. It will take time partly because of staffing levels and because adoption is not something to be undertaken on a whim. Once you have been accepted you will be asked to attend training courses to prepare you to be able to take a child within the age bracket you requested or is most likely to be available.

Needless to say it is not a shop window, and who you are offered may be totally different from who you were expecting. Children are not placed with adopters on the basis of who has been waiting the longest. The adopter must be the best possible match taking all the relevant factors into consideration, such as ethnicity, cultural needs, locality, background compatibility and much more. So much is done and so many factors taken into consideration to give the adoption the best possible chance to work to the benefit of the child. When you are thinking about adoption keep your mind and your heart open.

I have dealt with adoptions for all ages and I have seen many successful adoptions of older children as well as babies. Adopting is hard work and will have its share of heartache, however it will be one of the most rewarding things you can do. Giving a home to and sharing the life of a child is one of the greatest things you can do. Somewhere there is a child waiting for you.

5. *Getting Started*

There are many reasons why we choose to adopt another person's child. A common belief is that adoption is only available for couples who are unable to have children of their own. However in this modern day adoption is open for so many others including single people, adults who have children and wish to extend their family, same sex couples and older people. Many people shy away because they feel that by enquiring they are committing themselves. This can be no further from the truth. If you are not happy after making initial enquiries there will be ample opportunity for you to withdraw, without fear of embarrassment or recrimination.

Once you have decided to proceed with your enquiry, I recommend you look at your Local Authority website, and follow the links to Social Services, young people, fostering and adoption. There you will find all the details you need to start your enquiries. Or, if you prefer you can telephone The Fostering and Adoption team who will be pleased to talk to you. They will probably send you an initial enquiry form or invite you to an open evening. This is a social evening where you may meet other like-minded people and social workers. If this is not available, Social Services may send an adoption social worker to meet you for an informal chat.

They might offer you the chance of being a foster carer; this way you may become more used to caring for children. Many people who go on to adopt start out as foster carers. I have often been told by others that they could not stand handing the child back or over to someone else. I have been told I must be quite hard to do this. I can assure you I am not. Over the years I have taught myself ways to let go but that does not stop me having a few tears when the children in my care leave to go to their adopters.

From here things start to get more involved. Social Services will need all your personal and financial details and character referees will be required. You may find this very intrusive and feel they want to know very personal details about you, no stone uncovered, no secrets held. Try not to worry this happens to everyone who has dealings with Social Services children. They need to know you very well before you can be considered.

While this is happening you will be asked to attend training evenings where you will learn many things about how to care for the children. Here you will meet other prospective adopters like yourself. There is no need to feel you are on your own.

When all of these things come together your application will be presented to the Adoption Panel for approval. This whole process will take approximately six months. Once the application has been accepted you will enter into a period of limbo whilst a suitable child is sought for you.

You will be offered specialist courses to suit the age bracket for which you have indicated your interest, either up to two years, two to four years, or older. There will probably be courses on safe practice, understanding sexual abuse and understanding alcoholism. My advice is to take advantage, it does not mean that your child will have these problems and for those who have their own children, you may feel there is no need. I can assure you no one knows everything and it helps to broaden your knowledge.

As foster carers we have to attend these courses when offered and I can remember sitting there thinking that I had heard it all before. Then an issue was mentioned and I realised that it was something I did not know about.

6. Professionals and Procedures

I feel it is important to have an understanding of some of the professionals you are likely to come across in the adoption process. What I am presenting to you is a layman's guide and not a job description. I will only identify the part of their tasks that apply to you.

The Social Workers

These people are going to be a part of your life for a while. As I am now retired I can speak freely. Social workers as a group are just like any other profession; the majority do a good job and work under pressures that you and I may possibly find intolerable. They are no strangers to being in situations where they are damned if they do and damned if they don't. They can be in the wrong for leaving a situation and in the wrong for changing it. There are a few that are exceptional and few that are not. But without exception they all try to do their best for the child that they possibly can, within the framework that they are given to work, and within the budgetary restraints that are placed upon them. I have seen them work tirelessly trying to find the best match for a child who is to be adopted. Exploring every possible avenue or list of possible adopters searching for the best match they can find. So please remember that when they are working with you they are at all times doing everything they can to see that the match is the best for the child, and that the adoption will stand the best possible chance of being successful. Some adoptions do fail and that is a tragedy for all concerned, so limiting the possibility of this happening is their sole aim.

Their devotion to achieve what is best for the child becomes a personal quest that exceeds their allotted day. Sometimes this may come across as if they're being a little possessive of the child. Do not worry it will not go on for long. I will also add to this statement that you will see via the media, social workers made to appear completely out of touch with a given situation. It is a fact that because of privacy laws the social workers have no right of reply to these accusations at the time of the event. Whilst sometimes the accusations may be justified, there are other times when they are not. It is worth remembering that we can all think of things we could have done differently with the benefit of hindsight.

I have read an article involving a situation where I was the foster carer and therefore had much of the relevant information, the facts given in the media were from one side only, yet I knew so much more to be true. The social worker's actions, as they were presented, appeared to fall short of what was expected. However I was aware that if the facts as I knew them were to be presented, then the light would have shone in a totally different direction. So when reading such criticisms please remember there are two sides to every situation.

You will come to know several different social workers in the course of becoming an adopter. When a child comes into care they will have a caseworker who will guide the child until adoption is found to be necessary and approved. Social workers and caseworkers work out of an area office and are part of a team. Whilst the caseworker has specific knowledge of the child, every member of the team will have some knowledge and this is kept current by regular meetings. The idea of working this way is so that should the caseworker be absent for any reason, the remaining social workers in the team would be able to take over because they have basic knowledge of the child and family situation, thus saving any delays in keeping the case moving forward.

Once adoption has been approved the child's file is passed over to an adoption social worker. Adoption social workers work from a central office, and their aim is to take the child through until the adoption is complete. They specialise in family finding, matching and all aspects of adoption. You will also have an adoption social worker who will look after you from your first application to adopt.

All foster carers also have a social worker. It is their job to look after the foster carer's practical needs as well as their welfare and training; they will see that the foster carer's interest is being best served in meetings related to the children in their care, when the foster carer themselves cannot be present.

The Looked After Child Team (LAC)

These social workers are known as the LAC team, and are employed by Social Services but work independently. They will chair three-monthly reviews of every child who is in care. Everyone who is involved with the child is invited to a LAC review: birth parents, foster carers, health workers, social workers and teachers.

This meeting is friendly but formal and minutes are taken. The purpose of this meeting is to monitor the progress of the child and to see that all the targets for the development of the child are being met, plans for the future are worked on and every effort is made for the child to thrive. In this review everybody involved is answerable to the LAC officer.

When a child has been placed for adoption the child's birth parents cease to be part of the review, these reviews will continue until adoption is complete. Once the child has come to live with you these reviews will take place in your home.

Educational Support for Looked After Children (ESLAC)

This team, known as ESLAC, is not part of Social Services, but part of your Local Education Authority. Their role is to see that the educational needs of the Looked After Child is being met, covering everything from making sure they are in the correct class for their ability, to seeing if the child needs extra help with settling in. They visit the child at school and try to help them with one to one support if necessary. It is worth remembering that once a child is placed with you, and until the adoption is complete, your child will still qualify for ESLAC support and their assistance is well worth pursuing if your child is of school age.

Health Visitors

These people look after children from birth until they are five years old. They may come to your home or see you and your child at baby clinic. They are there to help and advise you on many aspects of caring for your child. Not only will they tell you when your child's vaccinations are due, but also they are an invaluable help in all aspects of childcare such as knowing where nursery and child play places are available. I have met lovely health visitors who have gone the extra mile for me and the children in my care.

It is wise to remember that health visitors are employed by the NHS and, like all employees of this service, they are sent directives on how to promote or demote certain practices with relation to bringing up your child. It is their job to enforce these directives, whether they agree with them or not.

Forensic Psychologist

Over the last eight to ten years a new service has been introduced into the Local Authority care system provided by a forensic psychologist. One should cast aside any misconceptions of the psychiatric profession for I have found them to be invaluable. Whenever I was concerned with any of my foster children's emotional or behavioural development, I would telephone their department and talk to someone. They would always listen, and then offer me various ways of dealing with any of my worrying situations. They would continue to keep in contact with me by phone to check how things were progressing, guiding and advising all the time. In extreme situations they would visit my home. This service extends to the child post adoption as well whenever possible.

There are three additional titles that you are likely to hear of in your meetings and reviews. Whilst it is unlikely that you will have direct contact with these officers, it is useful to know their function.

The Family Support Workers

Family support workers are employed by the Local Authority. They are fully vetted and are there to assist social workers at the practical end of the scale. This will mean anything from transporting and accompanying a child to school and contact meetings. They can go into the home and give practical help to families who are struggling.

The Guardian (Court)

The guardian is a representative of the family courts who will attend all family court hearings. It is their job to gather information from all parties including foster carers, social workers, birth parents and the children themselves. The guardian will then report back directly to the court with everything that they have learnt along with their own opinion. They are answerable only to the family court and must have access to everything regarding the child.

The Child and Family Court Advisory and Support Service (CAFCASS)

As the name states, this is an advisory service to families regarding all matters relating to the child and family court. They are proactive and in matters of parents voluntarily putting their children into care or for adoption, they act independently to see that the birth parents are aware of what they are undertaking, and to see that no undue pressure is placed upon them.

Procedure

It is helpful to understand the procedures that take place to cause the child to need adoption. It may surprise you to know that there are only two people who have the right to immediately take a child away from its parents. That is the police and a doctor; they can only do this if they have proper grounds to believe that not to remove would leave the child in immediate danger.

The usual course would be that a family who was causing concern would come to the Social Services' notice. Or maybe the family had asked Social Services for help. Alternatively, they could have been referred from nursery school, school, medical professions, police or even an anonymous phone call, which all must be checked out. Whichever way it comes the Social Services will instruct a social worker to call. Depending on the gravity of the situation, they will take the appropriate action. Nine times out of ten, this will involve discussing a situation with the family and making them aware of concerns. Only if there is a danger of physical harm, will they take more severe action.

When the social workers return to the office, they will write a report and discuss the case with their line manager. Once again, depending on the case itself, some form of physical help may be required and more inquiries will be made. The social worker will then monitor the situation and if no significant change is happening, and it is felt that the needs of the child are not being suitably met, the decision to bring the child into care may be made. This process starts with the Local Authority issuing the parents with a Letter Before Proceedings. This will instigate a formal meeting between parents, social workers and legal representatives. The problems will be identified and remedial actions will be agreed, with responsibilities being allocated to both sides. There will be regular review meetings called. If the arrangements are not met, the case will be elevated to the family courts, where care orders would be sought. There are several types of care order that the judge or magistrate can issue. If the situation that the child is in is deemed extremely dangerous then there are immediate procedures that can be taken to remove the child from the place of danger. Once again this can only be done with appropriate legal sanction. The point I wish to make is that Social Services never act without satisfying the court's instruction. It is the court that issues the instructions to the Social Services. Later on, if it is felt that adoption is best, then the Local Authority will have to return to the court for an adoption order.

Obviously there are systems available for birth parents who wish to place their children in Local Authority care and this is achieved by the application of a Section 20 Care Order. This means that the birth parents and Local Authority agree to the child being accommodated, and the responsibility shared. Adopters should not feel that that the child being presented to them for adoption is only there for minor reasons. They are in this situation because lengthy court processes have concluded that this is the best position for the child.

Once the child is placed with the adopters, it may be a few months before the actual Adoption Order will be approved by the court.

7. *Concurrent Carers*

Whilst writing this book it has been brought to my attention that there is a new process being floated concerning the care and adoption of babies and children under two years. The basics of this plan are that if you are proposing to adopt a child in this age bracket you can undergo training in the role of foster carer, which can take six months or more. When a child of this age stands a chance of being adopted, they will be placed with the concurrent foster carer who will look after this baby/child whilst the court decides whether the child should be adopted or returned to its parents.

During the intermediate period the concurrent carers will be working with the child's parents and will need to "support the birth family's efforts to regain the care of their child". However if the court decides that the child's parents cannot provide the security and care needed, and there are no alternative carers, the child will remain with their concurrent carers, who can then apply to adopt them with a reasonable amount certainty.

It is thought that the advantages of this plan will be:

1. It may speed up the planning for the child's future.

2. It could avoid the stressful upheaval for the child when moving from a foster carer to a new adoptive family.

3. The bonding with the new family can begin sooner.

4. The adoptive parents will be in a good position to understand the birth parents' background and struggles, which will be helpful for them and their adopted child to know in the future.

To be a concurrent carer you will need to be resourceful and emotionally strong. This plan will not be easy and in my view is ill conceived. In my opinion the benefits to be gained do not outweigh the emotional cost to the concurrent carer.

All would-be adopters that I have met are in some way desperate to have a child and because of this they will agree to anything that will remotely offer them this chance. Foster carers can take years to be able to deal with the emotional disruption, and in some cases heartbreak, of being parted from a child whom has been in their care even if only for a few months.

It can often take six months to a year or more before a child is free for adoption. As concurrent carers you will be expected to bond with this child even while they are still seeing their birth parents all on the basis that you "may be able to adopt" this child at a later date. This will only happen if there are no alternative carers i.e. relations who can adopt the child. I am concerned as to how you as prospective concurrent carers will feel if you are told after several months of caring, that this child is not staying with you.

I have counselled foster carers who were emotionally distraught to the point of being suicidal at parting from a child in their care. What effect is this going to have on an adopter who may have had miscarriages and many more problems with conception, only to have a baby/child to hold and nurture and then have the child taken away from them?

I have recently had a newborn baby placed with me for adoption and through no fault of any individual, but by pure natural process, the child was not free for adoption for two years. I have also had birth mothers of relinquished babies change their minds within the six-week period that the law allows.

The concurrent carer should also be aware that while they are involved with this process, it is possible that another baby/child already freed for adoption may pass them by.

I was involved in an adoption last year where we were in the second stage of handover, and I was informed that we may have to stay longer at the new family's home or even bring the baby back home with me. This was due to a handwritten letter received at the Social Services office from a relation of the child. The adopters were also informed of the situation. It was not until after a legal meeting the following day that it was decided the handover could go ahead. The emotional distress that this caused the adopters is not something I would wish to see another person go through. This harrowing situation only lasted 18 hours, but nonetheless was extremely upsetting and stressful for the adopters and their family.

From another angle I would question how this scheme will be interpreted by the Family Court. In my opinion and experience, the courts are meticulous in the handling and the hearing of an adoption order and have distain for anything that may pre-empt their decisions. How will they look upon the situation where a child is already living with someone who is to be a prospective adopter? Placing a child with a foster carer is purely on neutral ground. I do not think that placing a child with a concurrent carer will be seen as neutral ground. Most of all my fears are for the concurrent carers. I cannot see how this will work. I would also like to add that from the amount of telephone calls I have received from social workers, my apprehension and fears for this scheme are shared. There can be no doubt that reducing the amount of time a child is in care and the amount of moves that the child has to contend with is beneficial to all. It is the emotional cost for the adopter that concerns me.

I would really like you to think twice before you agree to this scheme.

8. Victoria's Story

Here we are going to have to use our imaginations. You have applied to become an adopter and have now been accepted. Four to five months have passed and you have been attending training courses on how to care for children between two and four years old. You are doing this because you have probably been told that this is the age group where you are most likely to be offered a child ready for adoption. Other than this life is much the same as it has always been.

First impressions

You have received a phone call from your social worker requesting a visit and asks, "is it okay if I bring another social worker with me?" All of a sudden there are two social workers in your lounge telling you that they have a four-month-old relinquished baby who they would like you to consider adopting.

A relinquished baby is a baby whose birth mother has decided that she cannot, or does not wish to, keep her child. This mother is 20 years old and notified Social Services of her intentions six weeks before the birth. She left the hospital two days after giving birth and has named the baby Victoria.

We do not judge this mother and we have to respect her wishes. Babies come up for adoption for various reasons. It could be because of mother's wishes, a judge orders it so, or may be because of a tragedy. It has never been part of my job to comment or form an opinion on the circumstances of the need for my services. My job has been purely to care for the physical and mental wellbeing of the baby or child that came into my care.

You are given a condensed history of why the baby is in care and relevant parental details. The baby is with a foster carer and is doing well. The social workers are now going to leave you to think this over and will get back to you in a week's time.

Everything seems so sudden, but I assure you it is not. A lot of work has gone on behind the scenes. When a council's adoption team is informed that a child is to be placed for adoption, they will hold a meeting where they review all the available history of mother, father and child. They note all the key factors and then search that particular council's database of available adopters. They will be seeking as close a match to the mother, father and baby as possible.

If no match is found they will spread their net to cover a wider area, often sharing a neighbouring council's data base. If there is still no suitable match, they will then go to the national database, checking all the time for matches in ethnicity, personal history and any other relevant factors.

When they have identified a suitable adopter, they will go quietly behind the scenes checking that all that the information on the database is still current and correct. If the proposed adopter is out of their area they will contact the adopter's social worker for confirmation of the details held on record.

Once this has been done, the file is passed along the managerial line for double-checking and for the authority to proceed. So you can see that whilst things may appear to have been very sudden, in fact a lot of work has been going on before you were informed. You were not some afterthought, you were carefully chosen as the best placement for Victoria.

Victoria and I

I collected Victoria from the hospital when she was two days old. As is often usual at this time, mother will have left the hospital. All that Victoria has are a few clothes and perhaps a soft toy that birth mother may have given her, her red book and hospital identity bracelets. Victoria's social worker would have been there with the official placement documents, which must be produced to the medical team before they release Victoria to me.

The red book

When a baby is born, the hospital or midwife starts filling in the red book. It is intended that this book stays with the baby for the rest of their childhood days. It will have details of the birth procedure and any drugs administered, as well as Victoria's birth weight, body dimensions and any details of the birth mother's known allergies.

This book is very important. Every time a health visitor calls, you attend baby clinic or see the doctor they will want to see the red book and in many cases they will wish to add their own observations, record vaccinations, weight and measurements. In fact a child's red book should be a complete chronicle of their physical development.

Memory box

On arriving home with Victoria, it has always been my practice to have a pretty or appropriately decorated box ready and waiting. In the box I will place any items the mother has sent, the hospital wrist bands and any other things relating to Victoria's birth. As time proceeds I will add other items to the box like first shoes, sleep suit, soft toys and photos etc. This will become Victoria's memory box and along with her red book, I will give it to you to keep for her. I will also have a hard cover book and in the coming days, will take photographs and make notes on how Victoria is coming on. This I will also keep in the memory box. The social workers will also compile a life-story book, but this is usually rather general. I feel that my little detailed book of baby's first few months is a valuable item for the child to have in their later years.

Initially I will be bottle-feeding Victoria approximately every three to four hours, day and night, getting her used to basic things like bath time and bed times and even at this early stage I am starting to establish a routine. Baby cannot properly see yet but I believe babies can distinguish shadows. She can also hear me talking to her. I will be talking to Victoria as I am carrying out her basic needs.

For the first six weeks after Victoria's birth nothing can be done because her birth mother can change her mind at any time during this period. She will have a social worker visiting her to check she is okay and no pressure will be brought to bear as to whether she wishes to change her plans. After six weeks has passed by the CAFCASS team will visit her. It is their job to make sure that no outside pressure has been placed on the birth mother, and that her decision is freely made. Only when this has been confirmed can the birth mother sign the official adoption papers.

Meanwhile, in the background, the adoption team has been working away, searching for the best possible match for Victoria. It is felt that between three to eighteen months is the optimum age for a baby to be adopted. So everything will be done to locate the best match within this time frame. In this hypothetical case, the best match is you.

I will be told that possible adopters have been identified for Victoria about two to three weeks before the social workers visit you. No specific details just that an appropriate adopter has been identified, and will be approached shortly. This is my cue to start preparing myself for Victoria to move on.

New family

A week has now passed since their initial visit and the social workers are back. You have had time to reflect and have decided you wish to proceed to the next step. You will be given a more detailed case history of Victoria's genetic past to review. It is possible that a planning meeting will be set up to which I will be invited to attend to meet you. I will bring some up to date photographs and will spend time with you filling you in with all the current details as to how Victoria is developing, what kind of baby she is and her little likes and dislikes, that have become apparent.

You will not be able to see Victoria at this meeting and we are not allowed to exchange personal and contact details at this time. If you still wish to proceed after this meeting the social worker will arrange your medicals. I will take Victoria to see the doctor for a detailed pre-adoption medical.

The next stage will be for your application to go before a Matching Panel, which you will be asked to attend. The Panel will consist of 10 or more individuals including social workers, health workers, foster carers, paediatricians and other relevant professionals. They will have read Victoria's files as well as your files. They will ask practical questions about you and your aspirations for Victoria. This meeting is held in a very friendly and informal atmosphere.

I would like to say that this is only a rubber stamp exercise but it is not. On some very rare occasions the panel may ask for further work to be carried out and in some extreme cases they may reject the application altogether. However in this hypothetical case you are successful.

This whole package is now sent to the Local Authorities Decision Maker for final ratification. This will take seven to ten days.

What you are about to embark on is a pretty unique thing to do. You are about to take on the life of another human being whose natural parents will not be there. You are going to bring this little one up as your own to love, nurture and care for and to share their joys, their sorrows, their laughter and their pain.

I think you are very special people. However there will be some who will say that it's not the same as being a natural parent and that you cannot share the same emotions as other parents. That is nonsense and you only have to ask any foster carer or adoptive parent for their take on this subject. You are about to become a parent, a mum or dad or in some circumstances both, the main difference is you are going to get four to five weeks' notice that your baby is going to arrive and not nine months plus as would usually be the case.

The day for the planning meeting is here. It may only be days after you have heard that the panel's decision has been ratified. The purpose of this meeting is to decide the exact date of the handover of Victoria from me to you. At this meeting we can exchange details but you will still not be able to meet Victoria. Over the next few days after this meeting the social workers will produce an introduction plan listing specific dates and times.

The start of introductions

At this point it has happened! It is real, Victoria is coming to you. I will by now have her sleeping through the night (lucky you). Her feeds will have increased from three ounces to six ounces. She is smiling and developing a little character of her own. She will be out of newborn baby clothes and will probably be wearing clothes for a three to six month old baby. By this time Victoria will have formed a bond with me. This is good as she is feeling secure and safe and this is how I want her to feel when I pass her into your care.

Some days after the final meeting the social workers will send out by post a detailed plan of how the introduction and handover will go. This plan will have everyone's contact details on and details of any emergency numbers that may be required. Here is a copy of the kind of plan that I have been used to working with. However it is to be borne in mind that this is only a guide and can be adjusted to fit around Victoria's routine.

The basic plan of the proposed handover

Day 1. 2 pm. You arrive at Jacqueline's home for general introductions. Today you meet Victoria for the first time and stay for about two hours.

Day 2. 7.30 am. You arrive at Jacqueline's home and assist with breakfast routine, stay three hours. You then return at 4 pm to assist with teatime and bedtime routine, and stay another three hours.

Day 3. 7.30 am. You arrive at Jacqueline's home to get Victoria up and give her breakfast, plus bath time. You then go for a walk, Jacqueline will come with you, and return by 12.30 pm to give Victoria her lunch and settle her down for her afternoon nap. You return at 3 pm and take Victoria out on your own for a little walk. 4 pm you return and give Victoria her tea and stay to affect the bedtime routine.

Day 4. 7.30 am. You arrive at Jacqueline's home and take over Victoria's regime until after lunch, and 1 pm you return to your home.

There will now be a period of reflection.

Day 5. 9 am. Jacqueline will travel with Victoria to your area and book into accommodation if needed. At 2 pm Jacqueline and Victoria will come to your home, stay for a cup of tea and leave at 4 pm.

Day 6. 9 am. Jacqueline will bring Victoria to your home. Stay for an hour then leave Victoria with you, returning at 6 pm to collect her.

Day 7. 9 am. Jacqueline will bring Victoria to your home, stay a short time and then leave. You are to return Victoria to Jacqueline's accommodation at 7 pm in her nightwear and ready for bed.

Day 8. 8 am. Social worker will meet you at your home. At 8.30 am you all travel to Jacqueline's accommodation and collect Victoria for the last time. The social worker will return home with all three of you and spend some time with you. At 9 am Jacqueline returns home.

Please remember this is a guide only. If Victoria's routine does not fit, we will rearrange to suit her. And do not worry; I would have assured you that I am always at the end of the phone, day or night.

There is a very important period on this list that says "Period of Reflection". During this time, the social worker will contact you to ask if you are sure you are happy and wish to proceed. If you have any doubts or uncertainties this is the time for you to raise them. A social worker will also contact me to ask if I feel you are managing okay and how Victoria is handling things. It is usual for a social worker to attend my home during the first four days to observe how things are progressing and again at your home.

Before the introduction, I would have sent you a handwritten diary of everything that has happened to Victoria, day by day, from the time she wakes until she goes to bed and everything in between. This will cover a period of around a week. I am not sure if this is usual practice, but I have always done it and it has always been well received. I feel it helps give you a mental picture of her routine. To the extent that within a few days you will be visualising what she is doing at any given time.

In order to prepare for Victoria to come to you I will inform you of the things you are going to need, for example, whether she is sleeping in a Moses basket or a cot. The kind of baby bath she is used to, what size baby clothes she is wearing and what kind of bottle sterilizer I am using. In fact all the things you will need to have ready for her homecoming.

Victoria is yours

The day has now come when you will meet Victoria for the first time. As you can see from the above plan, you will arrive at my home at around 2 pm and Victoria will be ready to see you. I will ask you to sit down, and then bring Victoria and give her to you to hold. I usually give her to the mum first and stand back as far as I can, but I must not leave the room and I will stay in Victoria's line of vision.

She will always look to me at this stage as she is looking for confirmation that what is happening is okay. Babies are fantastic receptors. Victoria may not be able to talk but she can interpret my expression and my emotions with remarkable clarity. She knows what is normal and when something is not and in these instances she will be looking to me for reassurance and sanction. You are naturally going to be emotional and I will have no wish to intrude. After 10 or 15 minutes I will suggest dad has a hold. Then we can have a cup of tea!

I will continue to give instructions and guide you through her routine in line with the introduction plan and I will gradually pass more of her care over to you. Over the years I have developed a technique where I stand back and watch from the side lines. As much as I am watching Victoria, I am watching you. If I see signs that you are feeling awkward, I will step in with suggestions like "how about doing it this way" or "why don't you try that way". One dad wasn't supporting the baby's head properly and I was able to lift his arm to show him how. A new mum needed to be shown how a cushion gives support. These are only little things but are so important in making you and baby comfortable. I will also be showing you both how to prepare bottles, change nappies and all the little duties that go to make up her day.

Although they cannot talk, babies do give out signals. A baby can cry in several different ways all carrying differing sounds and each sound means different things, for example, my nappy needs changing, I am hungry, or I have a wind pain. It will be part of my job to teach you how to identify these cries. In the first day or two you will not think you will get the hang of it, but what amazes me is that by day two or three baby will cry and adoptive mum will hear and jump up to say "baby has a pain I think its wind" and is usually rewarded with a large burp. These are signs that I will be looking, for you are becoming more confident.

Believe me these days will soon pass and if I have done my job properly you will be off home with a lot more confidence and feeling more comfortable. You are now entering into the period of reflection I mentioned before. Your social worker will contact you to check you are still happy and wanting to proceed.

The next day I will bring Victoria to your home and we will follow the plan through to its conclusion.

Over the next few days I will be leaving Victoria with you on her own more and more. Hopefully by now you and I will have come to know each other better. During the time I am at your home I will talk to you about two major points.

Looking after yourself

Looking after a baby or young child can be exhausting, but you must make sure that you look after yourself. As important as Victoria's routine is, so is yours. Keep up your normal standards; get dressed in the mornings as you usually do, try to prepare the evening meal and other chores in the mornings. I usually find it best to do anything I need to in the mornings, when baby is having a morning sleep. Then

I can rest when baby or little ones have their afternoon naps.

You were a couple on your own before little one arrived. Don't forget each other now. An addition to your family will draw attention away from you both and a little jealousy can creep in. Make time for each other. Evenings can be your time together, protect it and use it well.

I have always got my foster children and the babies off to bed at a reasonable time and resisted the urge to keep them up with me. Perhaps my bedtime routine will help you.

Bedtime

Over the years I have practised a simple way to get babies and young children off to bed. This works for all young children but you must start as you mean to go on. Make it a rule that once in bed they stay in bed.

Young babies can start after their last feed. Put baby into bed and close the curtains, blackout ones work well. Have a kiss goodnight and leave the room. If baby cries lift the baby out of bed to check for wind, make sure nappy is clean and baby is not too hot, they may just need a quick cuddle. When you have checked all these things, put baby straight back to bed. Do not take baby or your little one out of the bedroom.

If a night feed is needed do this in the baby's bedroom. Your little one will soon learn that the darker bedroom is for night-time sleeping. This will help if your baby is not going through the night. Just having this routine will soon have baby sleeping through.

Resist the urge to bring baby into your bed. It is not safe as you may fall asleep yourself. Babies have been squashed falling between their mum, dad and the pillows on their bed.

When baby is first home they may go back to waking in the night for a feed but this only goes on for two or three days just until they are more settled.

From the time a baby comes home to me I like to make sure that during the day we are not too concerned about noise, no need to creep about. Baby will then happily sleep when you are vacuuming or the washing machine is working. I would strongly advise you to carry this on when the child comes to you. Obviously you keep noise down at night time but even then there should be no need to tiptoe.

Preparing you for your new family

The following things I will be discussing with you are of a more practical nature. First, register baby with your doctor and he will instruct the health visitor to call on you.

Here is a list of equipment that you will need.

1. Up to four months: a Moses basket plus a stand. Check with carer what she has been using.

2. A cot.

3. Pram/pushchair. I have always preferred to have babies lying flat in a pram but you may prefer a lay back type

4.   Sterilizer for the bottles. This will be used until baby is six months. I like the ones that go in the microwave. Clean hands at all times. As an alternative if you do not have a sterilizer you can use sterilizing tablets. All you need is a clean bowl, make the solution up as directed, and immerse the bottles, teats and rings. You will need six bottles, but check with the carer as she may pass her bottles to you.

5.   Bottle brush for cleaning the bottles.

6.   Baby bath. Ask the carer what they use as I try to get my little ones into a proper bath by the time they are three months old.

7.   Car seat suitable for baby's size and weight.

8.   Cot-size sheets and blankets, which can be folded in half for use in the pram and Moses basket. Please be aware that a blanket folded in half is equal to two blankets. I also use a shawl for cuddle times and wrapping baby's arms in when they are a little upset and need to be comforted and contained.

9.   Quilts are fine for later but while baby is in a cot I think it is safer to use blankets, baby can get tied up in the quilt.

10. A cot mobile that plays music. Many of my babies have gone to sleep just listening. Or you may prefer ones that also have lights that shine pictures on the ceiling, ones as can be used for longer. The mobile needs to be kept away from grabbling hands, as baby grow.

11.   Two towels and face cloths. I like baby to have their own rather than share the family ones as I feel it to be more hygienic.

I always send the child with the current clothes that they have been using. Check with carer about the clothes. Use baby's own clothes because they find them familiar and after a week or two slowly introduce your clothes, mixing the new ones with baby's own ones.

In this transfer period it is important to continue with all the practices that I have used and not change them for at least three weeks after Victoria has been with you and then only very gradually. There is a lot for her to deal with in the change of carer, so it is best not to change anything else until she has settled in with you.

When I have left you it is natural that everyone close to you will want to visit and see your new addition. I will advise you to keep this to a minimum and restrict the visits to around 30 minutes with not too much passing her around. This initial period must be used for her to accept you as her new carer and keeping things as calm and controlled as possible will help her to adjust more easily. Therefore you should inform all concerned of your plans in advance so as not to risk offending anybody.

When clothes have been bought it is understandable that the giver will want to see the baby wearing them. By the time all this becomes possible it's highly likely that Victoria will have grown up a size. That is why I say not to encourage buying clothes as gifts. Try to suggest an alternative gift.

We are now at the evening before you are due to collect Victoria for the last time. The handover in the morning must be as brief as possible. Long drawn out emotional goodbyes are not to Victoria's advantage or mine. It is worthwhile to remember that babies and little ones have a fine-tuned way of locking into emotional atmospheres and they can easily become stressed by them.

Over the next days and weeks we will maintain contact and I will be on hand ready to advise you in any way you think necessary and until all your domestic support is in place.

9. Daniel's Story

In the previous chapter we looked at the adoption of a baby. It is to be remembered that not all councils work in the same way, but the basic theme that I have related runs throughout.

Let's look at another hypothetical case of a little boy aged 18 months when he was placed in foster care and came to stay with me. We shall call him Daniel.

Daniel's birth mother is a drug addict who has now gone missing, leaving him with her friends. They have called Social Services as they could no longer look after him. Daniel has an older brother who is called Marcus. He was born with neonatal abstinence syndrome. This is where the baby is born with a dependency and the hospital has to gently wean him off it. It is a horrendous condition where baby is in a lot of pain and discomfort. Once Marcus recovered, attempts were made to find relations who may have been able to care for him, all of which failed and he was eventually placed for adoption at 12 months old. It is worth noting that there is an increase in the number of children being born with this syndrome in relation to prescription painkillers. Daniel was one of the lucky ones and there was no evidence of any addiction problems.

Marcus has been adopted into a family where he is the youngest of three children and the adoption is going very well. The social workers have asked his Marcus`s adopters if they could have Daniel but they feel that they are unable to take another child. Social workers will always give priority to keeping siblings together whenever possible.

Daniel's arrival

Daniel was brought to me as a place of safety, whilst a Care Order is applied for. Social workers will try to find the birth mother to assess her situation. It is felt that due to her history of drug addiction that adoption may be on the cards for Daniel in the future.

Daniel presents as a sad little man after being handed from one of mum's friends to another, with no stabling influence. His life has little or no routine and his sleep patterns are all over the place. He is walking and can say a few words. He has no red book. The social workers have taken him to a paediatrician for a medical and the doctor said he has found him basically healthy, a little overweight and rather lethargic.

Daniel can wade through a bag Quavers very quickly and can drink from a bottle of Fruit Shoot. He does not know how to use a fork or spoon and his approach to food is, if he can hold it, he will eat it.

Over the next few days I will start to get him into a routine by getting him used to regular meal times and basic cooking. For example cereal and toast for breakfast, a cooked lunch, and a sandwich and cake tea. I will reduce his intake of snacks and pop to the level of an occasional treat. Just as important as the food is the timing of his meal times, trying to get them around the same time every day. I will start his day with a wash routine and end with his bath before bedtime.

I shall register him with my doctor who will ask the health visitor to call to see Daniel. Daniel is no stranger to the TV and cries for it to be turned on; I will be reducing the time that the TV is on gradually as it is a proven fact that too much television undermines the child's natural ability to outwardly communicate. In Daniel's case I feel that he needs to communicate more so we will look at books and I will read to him and talk about the story, we will also play games together. Television will be limited perhaps just for an odd half hour. I am trying to stabilise his bedtime; it's a little bit of a struggle but we are getting there.

After a week, the health visitor visited. She weighed Daniel and said she will sort out a red book for him. I have managed to get Daniel eating with a spoon; he loves Weetabix for breakfast, sausages and mash, and custard with cake for dinner. He is now happy to go to bed at 6.30 pm. I am supporting his daily routine with walks in the park, playing in the garden and special family time. He is now showing that he is tired and ready for bed at the appropriate hour.

It is clear from Daniel's first reaction to my husband that he is not used to having a man around the house, but he is now beginning to warm to the situation. He is following Roger (my husband) around and whatever Roger has, Daniel wants one too. Whatever Roger is doing Daniel wants to do it as well. I have had a little trouble establishing boundaries and found for safety's sake the outside doors had to be locked; he still has a very free spirit. Daniel has a beaming smile and is happy to see everyone.

Daniel has been with us for two months and he is beginning to shine a little. He talks a lot clearer and refers to us as Jacqueline and Roger perhaps not quite as clear as that, but he is trying. Meal times are less daunting and he especially enjoys when we all sit down and eat together.

Six months on

Daniel is a happy little boy, and loves his food. He has grown and lost a little weight. He is just gorgeous. He loves meeting our family when we go out together and go to family parties.

Social workers have obtained a care order and have also located his birth mother. She is living 60 miles away; she still suffers with her drug addiction and has a different man in her life now. Social workers have made several attempts for her to meet Daniel but so far she has failed to turn up. The council has now started proceedings for an adoption order. Most times at this stage the court will appoint a guardian who is to look after Daniel's interest.

Whilst the adoption order is being sought through the courts, the adoption social workers are able to start the search for suitable adopters and can go as far as identifying suitable people. But it ends there. They will not contact anyone or take any action that could be seen to pre-empt the decision of the court. This is known as parallel planning. Like all court processes, seeking an adoption order can take many months.

Identifying problems and causes

Whilst I have no concerns about Daniel's physical development, I have noticed that his little paddies are developing into tantrums. This is beginning to worry me as the tantrums are getting greater. In dealing with Daniel's tantrums I try to take no notice and walk away if possible, he comes out of them if no one is paying him any attention. He is only two years old and cannot tell me why he is doing this. He is having periods of bedwetting and this is upsetting him although I do not make too much of it. He has had a lot of changes in his life. I always keep a diary for Daniel mentioning his daily activities, hospital appointment etc. I do this for all of my foster children. When the social workers visit my home I always ask them to read and sign the diary alongside the date of the visit. I do not know if other carers write diaries but I have always seen benefits for having something written down. I have noticed that this upsetting period seems to happen after the social workers have seen him. This is not an uncommon syndrome. Daniel is beginning to settle and he is connecting the social workers with moving on. I will try to remedy this by informing the social worker of this situation and requesting that on future visits she devote her attention solely to Daniel and any further discussion of his case should be carried out over the phone away from his ears. I will also make a point of giving Daniel age appropriate reassurances.

Beginning the transition

I have found Daniel a nursery place for two mornings a week. He enjoys painting and playing and he is beginning to interact well with the other children. Daniel is talking well and is enjoying a stable environment. From what we can gather he has been living with us longer than anywhere else, and naturally bonds are starting to form. I am aware of this and although it is good, I must try to make him aware in an age appropriate way that his current situation is not permanent.

I have just heard that the adoption order has been made and was not contested. I can now begin to talk to Daniel about how lucky he is, and how he is going to have a lovely new mummy and daddy/family as appropriate. I will do this in gentle stages, sometimes using toys to help him understand what is going to happen. At the same time I will be monitoring his actions closely.

The adoption process will start as it did with Victoria but with a few minor adjustments. You as adopters may be asked to make a DVD of yourselves, your home and any pets you may have. This DVD will come to me via the social workers. I will sit with Daniel and we will gently explore the contents of the DVD, with me giving him help to understand it. As in Victoria's case this will not happen until after your application has been ratified. Daniel is now three years old.

During the handover procedure, meetings at my home will be a little different. We will be going to play parks, having tea all together and I will be gradually transferring Daniel's care to you. You will be putting him to bed at his usual bedtime. Once again I will be slowly passing his care over to you step by step. The point of this introduction process is not only to familiarise you and Daniel with each other. When he came to me he was traumatised, but now he is stable and used to our routine, which he can trust and in fact he has bonded with me. Therefore to see us all getting along well will mean that he will pick up the signals that I endorse this situation. This will help him to become more receptive to what is happening.

The same will happen when I bring Daniel to your home. I will make a point of looking at his bedroom with him and pointing out all the things I know that he likes, again refreshing my endorsement. It is only over the last 10 years that I have become aware of how important these little procedures are to the child. I will have given you several items belonging to Daniel, which I have secreted away a few weeks prior. When you leave me to travel home, I will ask you to place these items in a relevant position in your home ready for when we arrive. I can assure you that for him to walk into a strange home and see some of his possessions prominently placed works wonders in helping him to feel more settled in his new environment. Again we follow the introduction plan as we did with Victoria.

10. Mary's Story

So far in my stories I have looked at the adoption of a relinquished baby and a little boy whose birth mother suffered from drug addiction problems. Along with this mother, we can also include alcohol addiction as another reason for adoption.

You are probably wondering why there are so many children available for adoption. These children cannot all be from the addiction-based categories that I have talked about. You are right. To understand why these children need adoption, and how we can help them, we have to know how they came to be in this position.

Over the last 20 years the banner under which these children come to need care is neglect. There are many different terminologies such as, failing to meet the child's needs, abuse, failing to provide adequate care and many more. The number of children coming into care by way of neglect is growing year by year and is brought about by different factors, such as media awareness and everyday pressures on mothers and the situation they find themselves in. It is mainly single mothers who are the source of these children. I do not mean that all single mothers are lacking, far from it, the majority do a very good job of looking after their children. However there is a nucleus of single mums who find themselves in a situation that they cannot deal with and from my experience these mothers come from an unhappy childhood, very poor home life and even the care system itself.

Equally there is a generation of young men who come from very similar backgrounds and who are helping to fuel this small explosion. To these young men the act of fathering as many children as possible has become a badge of honour, a mark of their male prowess. Despite giving off signals to the contrary, they have little or no intention of staying in a permanent relationship. To demonstrate I shall call on past experience to create a scenario to illustrate what I am talking about.

As it could have happened

Mary is 17 years old and comes from a broken home; she has had very little life experience, and did not have a lot of schooling. Mary's mum managed as best she could but there were four other mouths to feed as well as Mary, and very little money for the family to live on. Mary's father left the family home shortly before she was born.

Mary meets an 18-year-old young man who showers her with the two things her life has lacked: attention and affection. Within a few months he is the be all and end all of her life and after a short time Mary finds she is expecting a baby! Mary's mum is not very pleased with the news and after many arguments, Mary leaves home to move in with her boyfriend. He lives in a two-room bedsit, nothing great, but to her it is a home of her own. Now that she is expecting, Mary will see her doctor, and has to attend antenatal clinic. Here she meets new friends and is suddenly treated as an equal by other expectant mums, some of whom will be out of her social circle, and who would not normally have given her the time of day. This new life brings Mary the attention she craves.

Her boyfriend is still very attentive, the pregnancy goes into later stages and she is now showing her bump off proudly. With this comes more attention mixed with open signs of respect, people open doors for her, offer her seats on the bus, ask how she is and generally show her a consideration that she has not had before. You can see how these positive reactions can combine to lift her esteem. She has a complete new world in which she is the centre of everything.

John is born

Mary's baby is born, a little boy whom she calls John. Mary loves the attention she gets from the midwife and nurses and she enjoys the time she spent in hospital. Mary returns home with baby John and is having regular visits from the health visitor who tells her how lovely she thinks he is. When she takes John out in the pram he is admired by her friends. Suddenly, and only after a few weeks, the attention bubble goes pop. The health visitor stops calling, telling Mary that she will see her at the baby clinic. Baby John is very demanding and cries quite a bit, and her boyfriend is fed up at being disturbed by the night feeds. He is staying out with friends longer and longer. Mary feels very tired and lonely, the only one getting any attention is baby John and that's only if she can get out with him in his pram. John is now three months old and Mary is at crisis point. She feels very insignificant and dreams of the time she was the centre of her world. It is not necessarily a conscious decision that she makes, but in order to get back to that world there is only one path that she knows, and that's to be pregnant again!

Crisis point

Within a month Mary is expecting her second baby. Her craving for attention is once more being fed. However a few weeks later Mary returns comes home after visiting friends only to find that her boyfriend has packed up and gone! Mary is very sad, but on reflection she realises that his affection has been wavering and anyhow it is a situation that brings open sympathy which is an additional form of attention.

Mary tries to cope on her own only to find an eviction notice (her boyfriend has not paid the rent for several months). Mary is devastated does not know where to turn. She tells her problems to the health visitor, who she sees at the baby clinic. The health visitor suggests they enlist the help of the Social Services.

In response to the health visitor's phone call, a social worker visits Mary and explains that she will be her social worker and another one will visit to see John soon.

Mary is told by her social worker that she will help her to sort out her benefits. They are also going to try to help with the accommodation problem. Mary has more people in her life and once again receives attention from numerous sources. The pregnancy goes well and this time she has a baby girl whom she names Alice.

Support worker

Mary returns home and is just about coping. John is 14 months and she has baby Alice. This is a very demanding task for Mary who is all on her own. Social workers can see she is struggling and put in a family support worker to help her. Her support worker will help with general chores, but their working hours are quite limited. Six months pass and the old demons start to creep back in. Mary loves her children but the craving for attention and affection is growing. Mary's friend visits and offers to babysit to give her a night out with other friends.

We must remember that Mary is still only 19 years old and she goes off clubbing with her pals, where she has a few drinks, and meets another young man who is black. They have a good night with lots of laughs and then go back to her home. Two months later she is pregnant. Mary tries to find the new baby's father without success, as she does not know where he has gone. The attention situation starts all over again and this follows the usual pattern.

Dual heritage

Mary has another baby boy, Joshua, who is dual heritage. Mary gives birth to Joshua at home and after a few more months she is now really struggling. Social services have taken care of her rent situation, but the accommodation is not big enough and she has three demanding little children to care for. Social Services receive an anonymous phone call saying that Mary has been heard shouting at the children, there has been banging and crashing and it sounds as if she may have been throwing things around.

One morning John is knocked down by a car 100 yards from his house. It is not too serious as he is not badly hurt, but he is taken to hospital as a precaution. No one knew where he had come from or where he lived. At the hospital John gave direction to the police as to where he lived and they go round to Mary`s home to find her. Mary had not realised John had gone out as she had been doing the washing and attending the two babies, and thought John was in the bedroom. Mary was very distressed; she did not know how it could have happened.

The police inform Social Services and they call an emergency meeting. It is their job to decide what to do next, it is clear that Mary's situation is deteriorating.

I have said previously that I do not envy social workers. It is their job to protect the children; they much prefer to keep families together wherever possible. However in leaving the situation as it is, if something else goes wrong they would be held to blame. If they remove the children, how long is this going to be for, and will things improve for mum? Do you remove one child or all three? Mary was clearly able to look after one child. In removing the children does it mean that she will not have any more babies? I have dealt with the adoptions of children, who were number seven and eight. One to six was already in some sort of permanent care.

As I have said before it is not my job to form opinions of the decisions made, which brought children into my care. The children had to be the most important ones to me.

At this particular time let's say that decisions were made to leave the children with Mary and to put in some extra support for her at home.

Legal proceedings

Mary has been served with a Notice of Proceedings and she has been told to appoint a solicitor for herself. I believe Mary would be entitled for Legal Aid for this situation. The meeting was called and the solicitors and social workers spoke about Mary's situation. Boundaries were set that Mary would have to abide by; the same applies to the social workers. Mary has agreed to comply with all that was said.

Mary was re-housed and after a few months she had another baby, a little boy named Nathan. Life was very hard for Mary and she was only just managing, things are once again reaching crisis point. Social Services received another anonymous telephone call. They were told that Mary had left the children on their own overnight, and after an investigation it was found that this was not the only time.

An emergency meeting was held and it was decided to apply for an Emergency Care Order. This was granted and the children were taken into foster care and placed with me.

We now have John age seven, Alice age six, Joshua age four and baby Nathan nine months old. The court will decide the children's future. Mary will have her own solicitor to assist her at the court.

Birth control

By now you are probably wondering why no one used birth control. As far as Mary is concerned it is the affection of the moment that she craves. Under any circumstances she would have complied. Most young men are clued up on the use of contraception, even if it is only for their own safety. Sadly there is another group of young men who I have mentioned previously who chose not to use any form of birth control purposely.

Why did Mary not have an abortion? The answer to this is simple; an abortion would have been self-defeating because it would have deprived her of her children and all the attention and respect from all the positive influences that the pregnancy had given her.

Why was Mary not sterilised? Compulsory sterilisation is against the law. Voluntary sterilisation would once again mean that Mary would be giving up the very vehicle that supplies her emotional needs of attention and respect.

In respect of long-term birth control, I offer this true story

I once worked with a social worker of senior years and she had built a system of really befriending her clients. She had seen so many of their children coming into care that she formulated a little plan, and persuaded her clients to have a yearly contraceptive injection. She would take them to the doctors to have it, treat them to lunch, and then put a mark in her diary for 50 weeks' time to remind her to do it all again. She visited her clients regularly through the year and lovingly referred to them as her girls. On one occasion I met one of her girls who felt just as loving when she spoke of her social worker.

However at a court case this social worker was viciously verbally attacked by defending counsel who said that she was compromising the women into having birth control and depriving them of the right to decide when they could and when they could not have a child. It was implied that this practice was against their human rights. I learnt that soon after this event, she retired. A good caring social worker was lost.

Into care

Let's look at things from Mary's children's point of view and how this could impact on you as an adopter. The children are with me in foster care. John does not know why they are here, he says mum never hurt them, she got cross at times and they were all very frightened when left on their own. John did not feel that this was any great problem; he assumed that this is the way everyone lives.

It is worth remembering that in the eyes of children, no matter what happens to them, their mums and dads can do no wrong. In fact they often put their mums and dads on a pedestal regardless of what may have occurred. From experience I have learnt never to say anything bad about their parents or put them down in anyway. This particular instance is a little more difficult to approach. When the children are placed with me and the core reason for them being with me was either physical or sexual abuse, or alcohol or drug related, the child would already have a point of reference from their own experience. In most cases of neglect, however, the child is not consciously aware of anything being unusual or out of the ordinary.

Alice is waking up at night with panic attacks and she will not go to bed without a night light. Alice and Joshua wet the bed often and Joshua runs around saying "Mummy gone, Mummy gone" repeating several times.

Nathan seems unaffected; he loves a bottle and has not been properly weaned yet. These children are bewildered; the life they have led has given them very few barriers. John is a little too old for his years, and he tries the best as he can to tend the other children. He would just go to the cupboard take a packet of biscuits and share them with his siblings; he makes them drinks of squash on his own without any help. His schooling has been erratic as it has also been for Alice. Joshua has attended nursery school occasionally, when the support workers have taken him there.

My first job is to assure the children that the situation they are in is not their fault and to explain that they will be seeing mummy again, and they will stay with me whilst everything is sorted out. I have always found in these situations I try to tell the children the truth very gently. Once again the first thing I will do is call on my old friend routine. I will be establishing bed, bath and meal times. The children arrived with a mixture of clothes in black bin bags. With all children that come into care and when they come to you as adopters, do not immediately replace their own clothing. It is best to just wash, iron, and maybe mend the clothes. Introduce new clothing slowly mixing new with the old.

LAC review

We have had a LAC review at the council offices. It has been decided that Alice and John will be transported to and from their old school for the time being. It was felt that to be in familiar surroundings with their school friends would benefit them so would being with teachers they knew who would help them. The head teacher was informed of the children's current situation. It was agreed that a place be found for Joshua at our local Infant school. Arrangements were made for the children to see Mary on twice-weekly basis in the local church hall. These visits were to be supervised, by this I mean that someone from the Social Services would be present to give Mary a hand and make sure the visit goes well. After the contact meeting the Social Services representative will write a report on how the contact with Mary went.

We are now four weeks into the children's stay with me. Baby Nathan is enjoying eating small cut up food. He can sit in the high chair eating with us. He only has a bottle at bedtime now as he can also drink from a baby cup. Their day will begin by getting up at 7.30 am, dressing and having breakfast. John and Alice will be picked up for school at 8.30 am. I will take Joshua to his school at 8.45 am with Nathan in the pushchair. After school we may go to the park or play in the garden, other than Tuesday and Thursday when they see Mary at the church hall. Tea is at 5.30 and we all eat together at a table. After tea the children watch the television.

Bath is at 6.30, then a story and off to bed at 7.00 for Joshua and Nathan. John and Alice go bed at 7.30 and 7.45 respectively. Weekends are varied with lots of family time together.

They are also getting used to having a man around the house. Joshua and Nathan giggle whenever they see Roger, and they both like to walk and crawl behind him mimicking his movements, then shrieking with delight when he turns around to catch them doing it. John likes having a football buddy with Roger, they play and watch sport together. Alice is happy to see Roger but rather cautious, although if she is frightened by anything she soon runs behind him and holds on to one leg with her arm.

I usually meet the children's mothers when taking them for their contact visits. When I first see them, mums would become very distressed, but after a while they settle down and start to enjoy the visits. The children are usually very pleased to see their mums.

A further five months have passed and it is time for the children's second LAC review. The reviewing officer is pleased with the children's progress. She sees the children individually for a chat. John asked her "when can I go home". A support worker has taken the children outside for a chat with them on their own. In the meeting the reviewing officer asked what the council's plans were. The social workers told her that they will be calling a planning meeting in the next few weeks. There is a little concern voiced from the social worker who has been visiting Mary. On two of the last three times she has visited, Mary has not been at home.

When the social worker telephoned Mary said she had not been well. On the last visit a neighbour told her that Mary has a new boyfriend, but when the social worker spoke to Mary she denied it.

Mary's attendance at the visits with the children has become rather erratic. She cancelled two out of the last five. On an unannounced visit by the social worker she met Mary with Joshua's dad. He told her that he has been working away and did not know about Joshua, it was obvious that he had moved in. Mum then went on to drop two more bombshells; they are intending to get married and she is expecting again. Joshua's dad is employed and has a good job. He stated that he is very keen to see Joshua and ultimately they would like to have Joshua returned to them. However it was obvious to the social worker that he was not so keen to see the other children.

A planning meeting was held and it was decided that regular visits would be made to Mary's home. Social Services will assess her and Joshua's dad and if everything proceeds well, Joshua will have separate meetings with Mary and his dad. Social Services will also assess Joshua's mum and dad together as a couple. Mary will continue with her visits in the church hall to see all four children together.

After about three months a further planning meeting was held. With reports from social workers, support workers and the health visitor, it was decided that as Joshua and the expected new baby would be full siblings and dual heritage, every effort should be made to keep them together. As a couple they were able to provide a suitable home for Joshua and the new baby. Plans were made for Joshua to return home with his mum and dad, and after a few more visits to the home, Joshua went home to live with his own family.

Decisions like this are not made lightly and the focus will always be on what is best for the child. An adoption order will then be sought for the other three children. They are planning to look for a family for all three to be together. So we now have three children to be placed for adoption: John, eight years, Alice seven years and Nathan 20 months old. Mary defended the Adoption Order, Joshua's dad did not attend. The court felt adoption was in the children's best interest and the Order was made.

From this story you can see how we can end up with three children needing adoptive parents, and how present day adoption needs differ from those 30 years ago when adoptions were usually focused on one very young child. I will add that this story is based on collective fact, and all other details have been changed. I am sure that this scenario is growing, and is not limited to one case a year per council. You only have to think of every borough in the country and multiply it by three to work out how so many children come up for adoption by this type of scenario alone. Finding a family for larger groups of siblings is no easy task and it can take time to sort out this situation.

New family

A family was found for John, Alice and Nathan with a couple who were in their early forties. They all went to live on a farm in the West Country. Off they went to their new family trailing their cases behind them, what a lovely picture it would have made. Children may come into my care with their clothes in a bin bag but when they left, they would always have their own case. The farmer and his wife had a grown up son who worked on the farm and they felt that they had room in their life to offer the children a secure home in which they could thrive. They had not intended to have an extra three children but after reading the children's file, they couldn't bear the thought of them being split.

Alice and Nathan settled down after a short time but it took a long time for John to settle. He was devastated at being, as he says it, rejected by Mary and although I had explained many times the role of foster carers, John asked several times why he couldn't stay with us. Gradually he settled down and found a friend in the farmer's son. The last we heard he wanted to work on the farm just like his new big brother.

Mary married Joshua's dad, the last pregnancy did not go well, and she was advised not to have any more babies. The two families will exchange visits twice yearly and all get together with all the children and their new families. The new family has accepted Mary and all seem to enjoy the visits.

We fostered a real family of three many years ago that were adopted by a famer and his wife. The eldest child found it hard in the beginning, but did eventually settle. The younger children were all very happy because they dearly wanted a new mum and dad. The adoption went well and I believe the children have all settled down well. Their eldest son befriended the oldest boy and the last we knew he had gone on to be a fully-fledged farmer.

11. Adoption Parties

All of the children mentioned were successfully placed for adoption by using traditional methods. If not, they may have just stayed in foster care. However there is a new method of introduction being floated, and this goes under the banner of an adoption party.

As an adopter you may be invited to one of these. Social Services will select suitable premises where they can bring potential adopters and the available children together in an informal atmosphere for a party. Here you can meet with the foster carers who have been caring for these children and their social workers who will be happy to answer questions about the children.

For the children this is a fun day with lots for them to do. It may be a fancy dress party, which you may like to join in. It is a good way for you to join in with their play and it is a relaxed way of seeing how the children really are. These children have been unlucky in not yet finding their own new mum and dad. There will be sibling groups as well as single children.

It has been reported that there has been some success with this scheme. There are disadvantages to be considered as the children have not been specifically matched to you and your family. You may feel it is like a marketplace with social workers trying hard to find placements for these children, but on the other side you would not have normally met the child/children until the first visit at the foster carer's home. This way you get a chance to meet the child and imagine how family life could be.

What also needs to be considered is how this affects the child who may have been to three or more of these parties without finding their new mum and dad.

This practice is constantly being reviewed and it is hoped that its full potential can be enhanced.

12. Behaviour

I am going to talk to you about how the experiences of the children I have been writing about is likely to affect their behaviour when they come to live with you. Please remember that every child is different and will respond to the experiences in a different way. Some may even give an outward appearance of not being affected at all. However it is best for us not to be too complacent for it is unlikely that their experiences would have had no effect at all. Whatever the outlook appearance it must have had some effect on them. The patterns I will describe are based purely on my own past experience.

First of all let's look at Victoria. She falls into the 0 – 6 months category. It is felt that this age group has the optimum chance of settling into a new family with no problems at all. I have been told that after a very short time, she should have no memories of life before coming to you. My own opinion of this is that whilst she has no conscious memory of the adoption, the fact that she left her birth mother, and then came into care to live with me, bonded with me and now, after some time, has gone from me to you, must impact somehow. The culmination of these events must have some impact in the building of her personality, even if it is only to the point of her making new attachments.

Daniel was 14 months and he had three homes before coming to live with me. He stayed the majority of his life so far (two years and two months) in my care and completely bonded with me. Now he is coming to you. For the first few weeks he appears happy. He will talk about me and make references to me and my family, but otherwise he seems to have settled. This is known as a honeymoon period. Regardless of what he has been told, in his mind I will still be coming to fetch him. When he realises that I am not coming for him, his behaviour will start to change. He is likely to have tantrums, and wet the bed even though he has been dry for a long time. He will push you away one minute then cling to you the next. It is not uncommon for children to regress when they change homes. It will manifest itself by making them behave much younger than they are. You will need all the warmth and understanding that you have. Whilst maintaining your boundaries and disciplines you must not stifle his behaviour. He will need to get things sorted out in his mind for himself and this will take time and patience. If you do it this way you will find this behaviour will gradually taper off. Home life will become more normal. It is not over yet.

Testing times

His behaviour may change as he starts to test your loyalties to him. He will be seeking to make sure that you are not going to move him on as well. Experience has shown me that, despite everything I did to reassure a child that they had done nothing wrong to cause the move; they still felt it had happened because of something that they had done. Showing warmth, understanding and reassurance is the best way forward. After a period of time he will gradually accept that he is now your child.

However there will still be incidents that will require you to think ahead as to how your actions will impact on him. You will have to be disciplined even to the point of not being late picking him up from school. Should this happen he will become very anxious and stressful and will begin to be concerned that you may not be coming back at all. There will be many of these types of hurdle to jump. For instance, you may be planning a house move, he will naturally become aware of this and because of his past experience will begin to feel insecure. Is the move going to include him? Is it he that is moving on? You must be prepared to share all information from day one. Include him and reassure him that you are moving as a family and he is part of it. I have known children to become troubled when packing up to go on holiday, reassure them that you will all be coming home after the holiday; we see a suitcase in one way, they see it in another. Generally, I think you should allow at least 18 months before he will feel part of your family. His behaviour will go in peaks and troughs.

Children of all ages will have the some of the feelings that I have just described.

Mary's children

For a child like John this change will become very difficult. He will not accept that the move was necessary and will have a mixture of emotions. John will wonder what he did wrong, why did Mary reject him? It will take time for him to move on and make sense of everything. He may well believe that this was his fault and will be inwardly angry and you will need to help John express this. Often with this age group the last person that they hold responsible for anything is their own mum or dad. They would sooner accept blame themselves. John may not have any trust in women at all. He will feel women have let him down; he will include me as his foster carer in this. The female adopter may find this difficult and upsetting but after a time if she can stay loyal to John, always being there for him, standing up for him when he is in the right and alongside him when he is not, then in time you will change this perception and John will become much closer to you.

Children like Alice who have moved with their own siblings settle much easier. She will share some of the feelings that her brother has. Alice will have the benefit and reassurance that an older sibling can give and being the middle child will help her to feel safer and secure. Girls tend to accept a new loving mum and dad much quicker.

As far as Nathan is concerned, I refer you back to what I have already said about Daniel. Warmth, routine and regular food will help. Nathan has his older brother and sister with him and the change will not appear so hard but it will still take time for him to feel secure.

As an adopter you must accept your child had a life before they came to you. Allow your child to talk, perhaps about when he was at his first home with birth mum and dad and when in foster care. Be open with them; if they need to talk let them. Children that have moved on from my home go with lots of photos, a memory box and a diary. Adopters tell me that the children, even after a few years, will still ask to look at the photos that I have given them and like to talk about things that happened especially about what's in the pictures. One of the adopters told me that if her little one has been reminiscing and seemed a little reflective, she makes custard and cake with sprinkles on top for him just like she knows I used to do and that seems to help. This may seem a very simple act and it is, but often the simple acts work best with children.

When young children came to stay with me, they would show exactly the same symptoms I have described. I would sit with them and let them talk about what has happened to bring them into care, chat about their mum, dad and any family. Whilst doing so I would ask them what little things they were missing like favourite food, did they like to sleep in the dark or with a low light on, and did they have a favourite toy. I would remember this and where possible try bringing these things into being over the next few days. This is all a normal part of the settling in process and you must not take it personally, even if it takes several months for them to come to terms with what has happened.

You may find that bed-wetting will recur. This is usually only for a little while, try not to take very much notice. Just quietly change the bed. The child may be embarrassed and not know why it has happened and may try to hide the wet bedding. I have found sheets under the bed, in the wardrobe, and even once out of the window lying in the garden.

I have had adopters telephone me in a very distressed state, and say that after four or five months their child, at times of stress, will still ask to come back to my home or want our car to collect them. I can only assure the adopters that it is early days and they must try to be strong. In time things will settle. Whatever happens, you must not feel that you have failed to make an impression. Usually by the time they telephone me again things have greatly improved.

I have recently seen one of my foster children who was adopted, and it is one and a half years later. I know he found things very hard in the beginning. However on this occasion I could happily see how well he has blended in with his new family calling them mum and dad quite naturally. He is truly one of them.

I have been led to believe that if a child has had a good experience whilst he has been in foster care; then it can take up to one and a half times the length of time that they have been in care, for them to really move on. For instance, if they had been with me for one year, it will take another two and a half years for their experience in foster care to move into the back of their memory. I have had recent experience with this and can confirm that theory is correct.

As an adopter you may find the settling in period to be difficult but like everything else the more you put in the greater reward, and it will come in time.

Finally, a few words about your own behaviour and how it may affect the children.

In our culture we can behave rather staid and do not openly show signs of affection to each other. When you have children that have had little or no experience of warmth and affection, it is surprising what comfort and reassurance they can gain from seeing you and your partner holding hands and the odd peck on the cheek. If this is not part of your behaviour at this time, then I suggest you give it a try. The warmth and security the child receives in witnessing these little acts is beyond price.

I can remember when the idea of group hugs first came into practice and I too felt a little strange when Roger called out at one time "group hug every one" at a time when a child felt distressed. We all ended up laughing and the effect on the child was quite remarkable. I feel it is all part of bonding together as a family. If you have any inhibitions in these little open signs of affection perhaps it is time to lose them.

Letting your child get to know you

While it is important that you allow ample time for you to get to know the child, it is just as important to allow time for the child to get to know you. They will be taking on a whole new way of living. It will be a different bedroom, their food will seem a little odd to them and there will be many new faces to get to know. Your priorities in behaviour and lifestyle may be completely at odds to what they have been used to; what in their past was taken to be acceptable may not be now.

Try to imagine the confusion they are feeling. Do not make their changes all at once; very gently introduce other people to them. If your child has been in foster care, be guided by the carer as she probably knows the child well.

It's a bit like baking a cake; you have all the ingredients in bowls on the work surface. You gently add one thing after another making sure it mixes well. Maybe you need to add more of one thing; you will know when it looks right. Slowly bake, checking the rising several times. This will give you a well-prepared, finished cake. If you throw all the ingredients in at once, giving a quick stir before putting it in the oven, this will lead to a disaster.

13. Adding an Extra Child to the Family

Adopting a child when you have already a child or children in your family is something that should only be done with a lot of forethought. In the first instance you need to be clear in your own mind why you wish to adopt. You will need to discuss this with your own children in an age appropriate way, well in advance of anything happening. Make them aware that their opinions are valued. Do not only discuss the advantages that you feel, but also highlight and discuss any disadvantages.

A lot of the adopters that I have worked with have had one child born to them and for many reasons cannot have another. It is not uncommon for the child to be the instigator in wanting a sibling. In these situations I have advised adopters that they should make their child aware of the changes that are likely to happen. Explain to them that they will no longer be the centre of your attention. They will have to share you both and everything that contributes to your life so far. There is no substitute for honesty.

It is also important to think about existing situations that you have with your own children. How you will implement them when your adoptive child arrives, especially in the early days? If your child is very young they may not have had to share toys before so your guidance may be needed. Please remember words and intentions come easier than deeds.

A family that I worked with already had a six-year-old son. This young man regularly went to football with his dad on a Saturday. They adopted a three-year-old little boy and I explained to them how important it was that dad continued this practice, so their son could still enjoy the one to one time. I also advised that as their bedtimes were naturally different they should maintain that gap for as long as they could to give their older child the security of feeling he is not losing his individuality in the newness of the situation.

It is natural for our own children to want to please us, therefore they will say "yes" or "we agree", purely as a reaction. You should give them time to find the words or show you signs that they are not really receptive to the idea. If this happens, it does not mean that you have to stop. Try to address the child's concerns and answer their questions about the adoption. Obviously if this persists you must rethink the situation.

Social workers will want to talk to your own children on their own as part of the vetting process. Their reactions and opinions will be noted as they will need to know that all of you are keen for a new member to join the family.

Whilst your children will not be included in the panel meetings, the social workers will present their report on your children's responses when they visited your home. Older children may be offered the opportunity to submit their feelings to the panel in writing. A lot of importance is placed on how your own children are going to feel about the adoption. They will be invited to the initial introductions at the foster carer's home but not usually on the first day.

In all families there can be an element of sibling rivalry and the initial settling in period in your home will be strange for all. Should things not go well at first do not panic; it will take time. However, if you feel that things are not improving then you must inform your social workers immediately. They will be visiting you regularly for several months after the placement and will have the experience, if necessary, to know when to bring in outside expertise to help you make all the adjustments required.

14. Post Adoption Contact

Several times I have referred to the 70s, 80s and late 90s, when once the foster carer had handed over the child to the adopters further contact was initially banned and more lately discouraged, other than the exchange of Christmas and birthday cards and this was only for a very few years. The procedure was not without reason. Adoption in those days was still predominantly for babies and young children and it was felt that the point of adoption was for the adopted child to be totally absorbed into their new family. The family would treat the child as their own in the literal sense. Therefore any contact with the pre-adoption carers would only serve to remind them that the child was not their own. It was thought that the child would forget their past life and their pre-adoption carers, therefore any contact with them would only remind them of their pre-adoptive life.

Now it is felt to be of greater advantage for foster carers to maintain a distant contact, perhaps meeting up occasionally with the child and their family. It was felt that it was not good for somebody who had been a prominent part of a child's life to suddenly disappear. In fact it has an adverse effect on the child's ability to make new relationships, for naturally they would fear that the persons they may become involved with could also disappear. It did not help the child to build relationship later on. In trying to bring about this change we are finding inherent practical problems. The main difficulty is to find a level of contact that would suit the carer, the adopter and the child. The adopter must not feel undermined by the carer and the effects on the child must also be taken into consideration. I have been carrying out extensive research into this and I am in no doubt that some form of contact is truly necessary. I would therefore suggest that all parties formulate and agree a basic plan along the lines of the following guide.

1)   There should be some form of contact after four weeks depending on how long the child has been in care, this could be by telephone or visual.

2)   After four to six months meet up again.

3)   Then again after a year.

Then if all parties agree contact can be continued. I really do believe that the adopter must control the frequency of these meetings, which should be held on neutral territory. Perhaps meet at a park or play centre rather than either of your homes. To the carer I would say I know how much it takes to part with a child but you must resist the temptation to over-impose on the adopter. In your heart you will want the best for the child, so you should embrace and accept the child's new family. I have now had contact with most of the children whose adoption I was involved with over the last 15 years. I was shocked at how the children still remembered me and were keen to talk about their time with me and my family. On at least two occasions this reintroduction was very timely as it helped the children involved make sense of some of their past. At the time of our contact, I learnt that some of the older children had been struggling. If we can get this mix right it can only serve to benefit the adoptive child in the long run.

One example of what I have been talking about is in this next story. I have changed names and other bits around but the basic facts are true.

Julie's story

There was an anonymous call at the police station and when the police investigated they found Julie in her cot all alone in a flat, mum was nowhere to be seen. Julie was in a soaking wet nappy, with an empty baby bottle by her side and bruises and cigarette burns all over her little body. Mum was not located for five days. She had been drinking with a new boyfriend and thought her neighbour was looking after Julie.

Julie was a very undernourished little girl when she arrived at my home, dressed just in a vest and clean nappy. I learnt that she was two years old, but as she had spent so long in her cot she wasn't walking properly. She was a very sad little girl who really pulled at one's heartstrings. She stayed with me for 18 months whilst an adoptive family was found for her. Julie was to be their first child and I knew by their actions that they would care and nurture her.

As I have explained before contact was not encouraged. I didn't have much contact when Julie left just a few cards and photos. Eight years later, out of the blue, I had a telephone call from Julie's adoptive mum and dad. There were no real problems, Julie had settled well and she was enjoying school with lots of friends, but they wondered if we could visit Julie or even just phone her. They had found Julie had been quietly looking at her memory box and she was rather distressed. On enquiring what was wrong she had said that she wondered how we were and would we have simply forgotten her. They had been talking with her on several occasions about her past life, and looking at the memory book. Julie did not appear have any memories about her life before coming into care and staying with us but her memories of us were still very much with her. The adopters thought it would be good for her to see us again, and perhaps an occasional visit would benefit her. I was very happy to agree to see Julie as I had often thought about her and wondered how she was getting on.

Julie was so excited when we called; she leaped into Roger's arms and gave me a lovely cuddle. She showed off her schoolbooks and several photos of her friends, who she named for us. We went to the park with Julie walking between us holding both our hands. On our return and whilst Roger was having a conducted walk around the garden, Julie's mum told me how she still takes the fluffy rabbit I gave her to bed every night. It has been washed many times. The suitcase covered with butterflies that she took with her when she moved on is still being used whenever they go away on holiday or stay overnight anywhere.

It was a lovely visit with us promising to visit again, which we hope to do perhaps once or twice a year, for as long as Julie and her family wants us to. I was so pleased to hear Julie calling the adopters Mummy and Daddy all quite naturally. Travelling home in our car I felt a lump in my pocket, Julie had filled my pocket with sweets and one of her photos.

On arriving home and reflecting on the day, we were amazed at exactly what Julie had remembered about us and our family. She was a little girl who came to us as a two-year-old, stayed with us for 18 months and is now 11 years old. Yet her memories were so vivid even talking about a holiday we had with her.

On telephoning Julie's mum after a few days, I was pleased to learn that Julie was much brighter since the visit and had an aura of contentment.

15. Parenting Pointers

I am going to talk about things you may find helpful. It is not a Doctor Spock style it is just some helpful tips that you may choose to use, but most important of all, it is to stimulate you into thinking how you may meet these challenges if and when they arrive.

Over the years many adopters have asked me what makes a good parent, I usually reply four things.

Warmth

By this I mean warmth of character, the warmth that comes with patience and understanding and keeping calm, when all around you are losing theirs. When you are snowed under with problems of your own, but you make your child feel that their problem is the most important in the whole wide world. By picking them up and brushing them down, by recognising when they know they have done something wrong and not giving them too much "I told you so". By not demanding gratitude, gratitude is a gift at the end of a long hard road.

Routine

From babies to teens every child that has been in my care has responded to routine of some kind or another. All children that come to stay have suffered some kind of trauma with adults. Because you have a smiley face and welcome them into your home, it does not mean they will trust you. Trust must be earned over an extended period of time. However to get them settled you will find that children respond to routine, to the extent that if you have established a routine and you intend to change it you must tell them in advance. When I refer to routines I mean having a regular time that you get up in the mornings and eat breakfast, go to school or nursery, dinner time, tea time and regular times for bedtime, even what time they have a bath. This will help them to know what they are expected to do at any given time. Always letting them know where you are, and what is going to happen next.

Good food

Still in an answering mode I will go on to bestow the virtues of a good diet and home cooking. I have had children opt for sausage and mash with a bowl of ice cream and chocolate sauce, against a McDonalds. However In truth I am getting a bit desperate waiting for someone to ask me about love.

Love

As an adopter, just like a foster carer, you do not have the natural right to receive love. Love has to be earned and it comes after trust. You cannot bring a child into your life and instantly say I love this child and he loves me. It takes time to evolve on both sides. By using one, two and three of my tips you will be off to a good start. There is no magic prescription to bring love into the equation just as there is no magic prescription for being a good parent.

I have been frequently contacted by adoptive mothers in a distressed state. They have had their adoptive child with them for eight to ten weeks and in some cases longer. Whilst there are no major problems they do not feel as though they have any tangible, emotional connection with the child. They are concerned that the child does not appear to have any feelings towards them.

The first thing to say is that this is not unusual and the best way to look at this is in the light of cold hard fact. From the child's point of view they have been placed with relative strangers and in a strange building, everything is different, even the way their food is cooked. They have been told that these strange people, you, are going to be their new mum and dad. It is a lot for them to deal with and it will take time for them to get to know you and trust you.

From your point of view as the adopter you have come to the end of a considerable period of vetting and processing. You have succeeded; the euphoria of success has passed. Here you are with a stranger in your home for who you are now responsible. You have to make decisions on a daily basis that are completely alien to you. It is of no surprise that neither of you are finding this easy. I reiterate; warmth and routine will bring you the responses that you crave. You will find that in time you will start to respond to each other.

You may find that this will be helped by natural events. Such as nursing a child who is not well or feeling very distressed. Make it easy for them to talk to you. I always found sitting on the floor with the child seemed to help them to talk.

One of my adopters who had all of the feelings that I have mentioned, told me how the child came home very distressed as another mum had told her off, accusing her of doing something she had not done. The adopter went on to say how all of a sudden she felt "how dare they do that to my child". She then marched round to this person's house and demanded an apology. On the way home after a mission accomplished, the little girl held her hand and smiled at her in a way that she hadn't seen before. From this time, their relationship went from strength to strength. It may not always happen with one instance like this, but it will happen at some point.

You will be inundated with "my children I did it this way" or "I did it that way". All you can do is listen, but you must make your own choices as to how you raise your child. It is also worthwhile saying at this point that a child's development is not a race. You will hear tell of "my son was walking when he was 10 months old" or "she could read music when she was three years old". Children will develop at their own pace in their own time. You can nurture and encourage but please do not turn their development into a game of excessive catch up. If you have real concerns talk to your health visitor or doctor not the next-door neighbour.

A point of truth is that I handed my last charge to her adopters recently. She came to me as a newborn baby. After all my years in caring I still learnt from this child whilst she was in my care. I don't think that as far as children are concerned you can ever know it all or know so much that you cannot learn some more.

Bottle verse breastfeeding

I think now is the right time for me to "get on my box" so to speak. There is a lot of controversy surrounding bottle-feeding for babies. So let's be clear. Mother's milk is best to give to your baby, if it is possible and if it is your choice. Breastfeeding however does not in itself make anyone a better mother and if a mother chooses not to breastfeed her baby, it does not make her a bad mother!

The manufacturers of formula baby milk invest time and money testing their products for the right balance of nutrients and vitamins that your baby needs to thrive, grow and develop. They get it as close to the real thing as they can possibly can.

I was not able to feed my own babies for physical reasons and obviously all of the babies that have passed through my hands have had to be bottle-fed. They have all thrived and met their milestones as per their red books. Many things come together to make a good mother and not one practice in isolation makes anybody a better mother that somebody else.

Crying baby

When you cannot get your little one to stop crying, their arms are flaying about and they are having a good yell, even the smallest baby can feel quite strong and awkward. Put baby over your shoulder and rub his back, once you are sure it is not wind and you have checked the nappy is clean. Place baby in your arms, wrap a shawl lightly across you and baby, so that the shawl or small sheet is floating free, and encase the arm that is waving about. Turn his head gently towards yourself close to your cheek. Hold baby firmly but not uncomfortably and he will settle after a few minutes and you can have a lovely cuddle.

Walking around often helps when they refuse to settle, as does singing to baby. Many of my foster babies went off to sleep with my renderings of songs and lullabies. I am sure you have favourite suitable songs and, perhaps, lullabies that you remember from your childhood. At this age the words are not important it is the warmth and tone of your voice that relaxes them. If this is happening at night I would once again suggest you do all of the above in baby's bedroom with a very low light. This all helps to get baby to realise that the bedroom is for sleeping in.

Bedtime for 18 months to 5 years

For trying to get children into bed and asleep in this age group I would recommend you try some of the following. All of this has worked well for me in the past.

Decide what time you want for bedtimes, remember children need approximately 12 hours sleep. New mums and dads have to work together at this time and put on a united front. It is no help if only one of you abides by the bedtime rules that you have set.

Blackout curtains in the bedroom work very well especially if it is still light outside at night and very bright early in the mornings.

If I have a three-year-old to foster, the child would have 6.30 pm as bedtime right from the first night that they sleep in my home.

6.00 pm.Give your little one a nice warm bath and get them into their nightwear, then perhaps a story cuddling up on your settee or sitting with the child in bed and you sitting by the side of the bed. This will help to slow things down and hopefully they will be sleepy by then.

6.30 pm.Put into bed if not already there, turn out the light, close curtains, say goodnight and leave. You may like to use a night light, they are very low lights but some children get comfort from them. Others like to sleep in the dark.

If the child is distressed go back for a quick cuddle but they must stay in bed and not come out of the bedroom. If little one is still calling out, do not waver; re-affirm the situation with a firm voice. If they keep coming out of their bedroom, a stair gate might help. They must learn that they are to stay in their room at bedtime.

You need to both be strong at this time. Don't get cross, talk in a calm voice, Stay calm and in control ignore any pleading faces.

I have found that children soon get used to this routine. Even when they come to stay and have been used to staying up late, I start as I mean to go on, it may take a few days, but they soon get used to bedtimes. It is really a case of standing your ground. Do not use bribes and promises; you will be making a rod for your own back.

A general rule with children of all ages is not to make idle threats. If you are not prepared to follow through with what you have said, don't say it at all. Children respond well to routine, it helps them to feel secure.

If your child has been in foster care I hope bedtime has already been established. Confirm this with your child's foster carer.

Calling you Mummy and Daddy

When your child/children come to live with you at any age, I know you will long for them to call you Mum and Dad. My advice is not to expect it to happen immediately but it may do. Depending on the little one's previous life they may be only too aware that they had another Mum and Dad before. Do not try to force the issue; the trauma of the move will need to be addressed first.

It will help if you refer to yourselves as Mum and Dad, for instance; Dad may say "ask Mum to do that". It will happen sooner if you have other children in your home, who naturally refers to you as Mum and Dad, your new child will want to belong and when they hear others calling you Mum and Dad they will want to join in.

If your new child is very young I expect them to call you Mum and Dad much sooner but older children will only do it when they are ready to and it is usually when you least expect them to.

Being a foster carer it was not my wish for children to call me Mum, we were always Jacqueline and Roger, but if they stayed a long time and were not going back home, it was what they would choose to do. I would try not to encourage this. If the child was going for adoption, I could talk about them having a new Mummy and Daddy of their very own.

Your new child will want to belong, so if it does not happen straight away, do not worry it soon will and it will be magic!

Disagreements

People have told me that they never argue in front of the children. If necessary they wait until the children are in bed and cannot hear. As a result of the argument the next day they don't talk to each other, and this creates an atmosphere. This is a case of giving with one hand and taking with the other. The child has not had the distress of the argument but will pick up the fragile atmosphere the next day. This is likely to cause the same distress as if the child had heard the argument and it will upset them just as much. The child cannot understand why there is an atmosphere and they blame themselves. We all have disagreements in all families and the best idea is to keep it out of the way of the children and no matter how you feel towards each other in the morning please put on a united front.

Open displays of affection such as a quick peck or cuddle or holding hands, is a very easy way of giving younger children a sense of wellbeing. Older children might look embarrassed, but they too will still receive the signal that all is well.

Meeting birth parents

In the modern adoption process you will be encouraged to meet at least one of the birth parents. The reason for this is to give the parent the opportunity to have a visual impression of the people who will be adopting their child and to have an idea of the kind of people you are.

This is an extremely emotional experience for all concerned. It is best for you to attend this meeting with an open mind and to forget anything you have been told about the reason for the adoption. You will feel a certain amount of gratitude to this parent for without them your dreams would not have been fulfilled. You may have sympathy for the birth family, but it is important that in this emotional meeting you do not make promises or commitments about the child's upbringing, which you will not be able to fulfil.

You will have been told of what is known as "letterbox contact." The birth parents are not allowed to have your address, so there is a designated address where, once or twice a year you will be asked to agree to write and send a brief resume of how the child is developing. In turn the birth parent is allowed to write to their child. The administrators at the letterbox centre will then redistribute the letters accordingly. It will be up to you to choose an appropriate time to give or read these letters to the child. The worst thing that you can do is to withhold the letters and I would suggest you save the letters after they have been read, you never know if they may be wanted when your child gets older.

Setting boundaries

It is as well to discuss what your boundaries are going to be, and what you are going to use as the consequences before the children have arrived. I say this because from the start you must both be singing from the same song sheet. Whether singly or together consistency is most important. There is no point if one is strong and one is weak, children are very cute at working this out and taking advantage. When the children arrive you must make them aware of your boundaries as soon as possible. This does not mean that you should meet them on the door step with your hands on your hips saying, "Right this is how it is going to be".

You should gradually introduce your boundaries in the first week or so. In an age appropriate way explain what you expect and why. The children will feel happier knowing what is expected of them. You must think about the consequences very deeply for you must be prepared to follow through. With younger children no more sweets today must mean exactly what it says. When dealing with an older child there is no point in saying "you're grounded for the rest of the day" on a day when you are all going out. The only one being punished is you. Whatever you do you must carry it out or it will become meaningless. One last thing, please do not join the "if you do it again" brigade and continually say it, but do nothing. By this I mean if you say "I will take your sweets away" then do it. Endless threats are useless and are no benefit to anyone.

Getting them involved

I have always believed that getting children involved with the everyday things in the household is not a bad thing. If carried out in age appropriate way it can be a quite fun thing to do and will give the child a sense of purpose and a feeling of belonging. Young children love to help and many of my little ones ran behind me with a duster, and even quite young ones enjoyed emptying the washing machine with me. They like to help to make cakes and jellies with you too.

Roger would often say to young boys "I would really be grateful if you give me a hand with small tasks". Then in the evening make a point of saying how grateful he was for the help and how well they had done. This helps build their self-esteem and sense of self-worth. It will make them feel very good about themselves, and you can see them getting all pumped up. It is all part of family life and helps build self-esteem.

Special times

In these materialistic days I would like to say that it is not necessary to build too much into what children enjoy. We are all aware of the one-year-old baby who on their first Christmas enjoys the wrapping paper more than the presents that they came in it. The two-year-olds who gets hours of enjoyment out of the big box rather than the toy that came in it. We can, if we are not careful, over bake these things. In my experience one of the main examples of this is days out.

I have spent days at theme parks and spent a small fortune. I did not mind this as the children were enjoying themselves. I have also, on the spur of the moment, decided to make a pack up lunch and go off to the seaside for the day. We would spend ages going round rock pools with nets and jam jars, have a dip in the sea, and a bat and ball on the beach, then a singsong in the car on the way back.

My point is the children will talk about the theme park for a few weeks. They will talk about the days at the beach or the picnic in the park forever. I recently met a young man who I fostered when he was five. He asked if I could remember the lovely days we used to spend at the beach. I know we also went to theme parks but it was the beach he remembered. He clearly had fond memories of these times and they had stayed with him, all these years.

16. Children Needing Extra Care

Sexual and physical abuse

We are constantly being made aware through the media of the horrendous effects that these acts can have on the victim. Children suffering this kind of abuse come in all ages, but whatever their age they all need special attention. They have lost trust in adults and must be treated with special awareness. They will see danger in everyday routines, such as bath times and bedtimes even to the extent of being a bit fearful of being left alone with an adult. Sometimes the abuse that they have suffered will leave them with an inappropriate way of showing affection and you have to direct them to what is, and what is not, acceptable without damaging their self-esteem, which will be very low. Perpetrators of the abuse usually make the victim believe that they were the instigator of the event, to such a degree that the child believes that they were to blame. Therefore they will have very little trust in their own judgment.

Children who have suffered physical abuse can present problems with everyday routine and discipline. They are used to having boundaries enforced with violence therefore routine punishments will not have the necessary affect. I have found that these children do respond to consistency of boundaries and consequences supported by the fact that you mean what you say. It will take them a long time to accept that you will not use physical acts against them. One of the most common problems you will encounter with these children is that they will cower at the sight of anyone raising their arm or moving quickly around them. It will take you time to get used to this so support your actions by giving the child continual reassurance they have nothing to fear from you.

I could go on to say more about how you can help the children come to terms with what has happened. I have worked with many of these children and have seen how they can be helped to manage their bad memories and the consequences that they have been left with. They can and must be helped. Each child will have specific problems so it would be wrong to generalise and you will need outside professional assistance to work with them. The professionals are brilliant at tailoring their guidance to suit the individual child.

To adopt a child who falls into either of these categories you will need to be especially dedicated. You will be given every guidance and assistance in understanding how their world has been and how you can help build their trust in you and, gradually, other people.

Neglect and emotional abuse

I have joined these two together as I feel that they merge. A lot of the children I have fostered come under this category. It is hard to find appropriate words to describe neglect. We seem to be able to perceive it in other countries through charitable advertisements on the television. We have all seen the pictures of little children in Romanian orphanages. What we do not grasp is that there are children in our country who suffer in a very similar way.

When we see neglected children in our country, many people assume that they only need a wash, change of clothes and good feed, to sort them out. Sadly this is so far from the truth. The best way I can find of describing neglect is to say it is the "persistent denial of responsive care". In usual circumstances a baby cries and we respond by going to see what is wrong. If a child is hungry we respond by feeding them. If a child is hurt they put their arms up and we respond by picking them up. For a neglected child none of these responses happens. They cease to cry because they know that no one will come. They don't expect food as it won't come, and so they will just grab and take what they can. They no longer put their arms up as they do not expect to be picked up. I have used these extremes to describe my views of what neglect is, but I am sure you will agree that even if I am only half-right neglect is something we should all be aware of.

Recent studies by neuroscientists have revealed there are not only emotional consequences to neglect, but the brain in a neglected child does not develop as fast or in the same way as that of a normally brought up child. If neglect goes unchecked the damage will be permanent and the child will become an adult with little or no chance of living a normal life. They will lack the ability to build stable relationships and most damaging of all will be their lack of empathy. The good news is that if we can get to the children soon enough and remove them from their neglectful environment, there is a very good chance their prospects may be reversed, but it is not certain. Once again this will depend on the depth of the neglect and how long the child had to endure it. By giving them a normal loving environment and consistency of care their life and their prospects can be greatly improved. This is where you as an adopter come in. What you can give to the child is desperately needed.

The children in this group are not always aware that there has been anything wrong in their upbringing. What is deemed neglect to us is normal to them. Therefore they are at a loss as to why they are in this situation. Children who have suffered emotional abuse are often withdrawn and overly compliant. They can appear to be very well behaved children and very ready to please you.

The lack of an obvious reason for their situation makes this group more likely to blame themselves for being in need of care. They feel that it must have been something that they have done. All children, other than babies, that come into care have one symptom in common: they all have low self-esteem. This will need a lot of pro-active building up and re-assurance, which will take time. It is very difficult to generalise the kind of behaviour to expect from these children, because it will depend on how extreme their situation was.

You must make sure that the social workers give you full details of these children's background. It is highly likely that you will be invited to attend a course giving guidance on the best way to help them. My advice would be to obtain details of the support the course offers. You should expect to be offered post adoption support, even if you have to ask in writing for details of the support being offered.

I have fostered children in this category and some of them were families of several children. The eldest who may only be young themselves, would have been responsible for feeding and looking after their siblings. When they came into care they would find it hard to let grownups take over.

I cared for a family of three children, the eldest was only four years old and her brothers were two years and 12 months. She would push me out of the way when the baby needed a clean nappy or when I tried to feed him. She found it very hard to accept that I was going to do it. It was obvious that this child was far too old for her years and was missing out on her own childhood. It took quite a while for her to let me take over the role of being mum to them all.

Another little girl came to me when she was two and a half years old. She stayed two weeks then returned home. Three weeks later she was back again. This little girl had had seven homes before coming to me. She was passed between neighbours and friends, never staying very long anywhere. She was very quiet, just sat on the floor. Didn't play with the toys, in fact she never spoke. After a few weeks in my care, she still would not talk to me just grunted when she wanted something. I noticed that when my own daughter came home from school, the little girl would quietly talk to her as if in a whisper. Time passed and she was happy to eat meals with my daughter, but still not talking to anyone else.

A few days later a bright bubbly little girl came to be fostered with us, she was three years old and would not stop talking and making everyone laugh. I could see the little girl eyeing her up in puzzlement. Within a week she was talking too, the two of them became friends and played happily together. She was adopted after another year had passed, the other child returned home.

I later learnt that although she was not academic, and she was never completely able to make up those lost early years that she suffered from neglect, and because of this she didn't do well at school. What she did have was a tremendous ability with her hands and the age of eight, she was repairing the bikes of children much older than herself. She transferred this ability to motor mechanics. This little girl also had a natural bent with art.

I have seen how children can be lifted out their old world and helped to adjust to a new one. Like many things in this life, what starts off being hard can often turn out to be one of the most rewarding things you could have ever done. It always gladdens my heart when I meet or hear about all these children and how their life has changed.

Jacqueline Hearn MBE

Children with special needs, learning difficulties or physical disabilities

To try to advise you about adoption of children who fall under this category would take a book in itself, mainly because there are so many variations in the need of specialised care that the child will require. This should in no way put you off from considering children who fall under this category.

You will be given full details of the child's personal and behavioural history. This will be followed up by a visit to a relevant paediatrician who will discuss the working implications of adopting the child and the likely ramifications and outlooks for them. Should you wish to continue then a support network will be put in place to assist you in every way. If the child needs personal equipment, then this will be supplied. It may be that you will qualify for additional allowances and you will be guided through this minefield.

I would never underestimate the hard work that caring for these children requires. But like so many things in this life, the more you put in the more you get out. There is one certainty in this field and that is caring for these children can be one of the most rewarding things you will do. Often their laughter and smiles have to be physically earned but it is well worth it.

When a child has learning difficulties it does not mean that they cannot learn. It means that they will need extra help and understanding to enable them to learn and this will be at a slower pace than normal. Do not be put off by labels and look at the children themselves.

I fostered a Downs Syndrome little girl for a short time as a respite. Her mum had to go into hospital and had no one to care for her child. It was in my early days as a foster carer and I must admit I was a little apprehensive at first, but at the end of her eight-week stay I would have loved to have kept her. Her little smile was delightful and the warmth that she generated was priceless.

17. Black and Dual Heritage Children

Until the 1990s the fostering and adoption of children in this category was not felt to be exceptional and it was quite commonplace. If the foster carers and adopters were happy to take the placements, there were no particular problems with mixed families. As foster carers you were encouraged to teach the children about their origins and make them aware of customs and practices suited to all sides of their background. In practice taking mixed race and black children into your home was only likely to cause problems in the eyes of those around you. As someone who has cared for a lot of these children and along with other carers in the same circumstance, we all just got on with it. For us it has always been the child who is important.

In the wake of the Cleveland inquiry, it was felt that the whole area of fostering and adoption had to change. The Cleveland situation arose when a group of social workers took it upon themselves to put several children into care on the suspicion that they were being subject to sexual abuse by their parents, and friends of their parents. It was later found that the whole case was not true but by then it was too late.

In light of this and some other high profile situations it was felt that the whole area regarding children in care had to change. As part of this change it was felt that black children should be placed with black foster carers and adopters, the same would be applied to mixed heritage children. In a nutshell, it felt to me as if it was being said, if you are black you're black, if you are dual heritage you are also black. It was claimed that if you were a dual heritage child your interests were not best served by being placed with a white foster carers or adopters. This theory was carried to the extremes.

I was involved with a case where a child was born with a black absentee father, a white mother and a white older brother and she had lived with her mother and brother as part of a white family all of her life. Sadly her mother died unexpectedly, her brother who was nine years old went to live with an uncle. The little girl who was eight years old needed to go into care as there was no one to look after her. It was felt that adoption was the best way forward for this young girl and, along with the new guidelines, a black family was found for her. The authorities failed to accept that the child had lived as part of a white family for all of her life. Sadly the adoption broke down after two years. She could not settle and I know she ran away several times, because she could not adapt to this large change to her lifestyle.

I went on record several times disagreeing with this theory. We all have our own heritage and I believe mixed heritage children and adults have two lines to their origins the same as everyone else. Just because they may involve different continents neither should be deemed more important. Through my dealings with other foster carers and foster carer associations, I was also aware that it was a fact of life at that time, that there were far fewer black and dual heritage foster carers and adopters in the system than there were children who needed care. I could envisage social workers trying to comply with the guidelines set out at that time, and simply not having enough suitable placements. This would mean that a lot of these children would be placed in care, in situations that were to be felt unsuitable. I take no pride in saying that my fears were well founded.

Around 2009–10, this divisional practice was reversed. Now when black and dual heritage children come into care, every effort is made to find the best match possible to meet the child's natural heritage. Priority is given to finding the most suitable placement available. The same happens when a child is placed for adoption.

Today we live in a multi-cultural society and emphasis is placed on whether the foster carers and adopters are prepared to embrace the child's heritage and cultural needs. Compared to the 60s we have come a long way. It is sad to say that we are not quite there yet and if it is your intention to foster or adopt black or dual heritage children there are things of which you should be aware. Some of them are very basic such as:

Looking after their skin

Black and dual heritage babies and children often get a white sheen on their skin and you only need to wipe gently with baby oil to get rid of it. When the child is older coconut oil will work wonders.

If their hair is tight and very dry, a lanolin treatment is needed. In my experience I have always found that Afro hairdressers are usually prepared to offer help with practical advice regarding skin and hair treatments.

As well as having three of our own children, we also adopted three dual heritage children who have all grown up now. When our adopted twin girls were little, Roger spent many, many hours sitting in Afro hairdressers whilst our little girls had their hair braided and beaded.

In the sunshine children with dark skins need just as much sun cream to protect them as white children; they can burn just as easily.

Thick skin

These days there are still people who believe that it's not normal to see a black child with white adults, and unfortunately sometimes you will need a thick skin. You must be prepared to receive enquiring glances and inappropriate comments.

I can remember on several occasions, passers-by who did not know me saying "You should be ashamed of yourself", as they walked off, and then at another time "did you sleep with a black man"? When out with the children I would see people I knew approaching me, and they would cross the road only to cross back again when they had passed. Some people you consider to be friends will all of a sudden stop calling round for no apparent reason. These examples are a little rarer now but nonetheless they still may happen and you should be prepared.

One day, I found a little boy I was fostering, in the bathroom rubbing talc all over his black body. Later I discovered that whilst he was at school other boys had said he looked like he had been playing in poo. This little boy was very distressed and I could only comfort him and tell him how silly I thought the other boy had been. We must not condemn the other children too much. For at a young age children speak as they see, there is no malice intended. Young children tend to accept things as they are; it is usually adults who install prejudice into the equation.

This highlights another area in which you will have to be extremely vigilant. I have previously said how all children in care suffer with low self-esteem, none more so than black and dual heritage children. They will need a lot of lifting up, maybe by looking for other role models suitable for both sides of their heritage. They will only be too aware of the negatives; it is up to you to highlight the positives.

Sometimes the positives will come naturally. I remember when we all had our first holiday in Majorca. My own adopted children who are dual heritage were so surprised to see lines and lines of people on the beach all sunbathing. When they asked me what these people were doing I was able to say that they are all trying to get the same colour skin as you. The look of pride on their little faces was lovely.

I would suggest if you are a white family considering adopting a black or dual heritage child, you should make your own children aware of the possibilities of the stories I have mentioned. They may also suffer a little fallout from the situation.

These observations are in no way intended to put you off. I only want to make you aware of the kind of things you may come across. In the last couple of days whilst I have been writing this section, I have received a telephone call from a social worker asking if I could have a chat with a white couple who were preparing to adopt a dual heritage child that they were fostering. The social worker felt that the couple were fine to adopt the little girl but had not quite grasped the possible consequences of what they may face. I also received a call from an adoptive mother thanking me for the advice I had given her. They had just had an incident with their dual heritage child and, whilst it was unpleasant at the time, they were at least prepared for it and that is all I try to do.

I have heard of a family, who have dual heritage children, they have started a gathering of other families of black and dual heritage children. They all meet together monthly, the children have a fun time together with friends of the same multicultural backgrounds, their mums and dads have a good chat. This type of get together helps with any feelings you may have of being on your own and it is so good for the children to mix with other children of the same colour. Something like this arrangement is of great use if you live in an area that is not ethnically diverse.

18. Teenagers

When children over 12 need care it is felt that adoption does not really fit the bill. There will always be exceptions to this rule, but it is felt that long term or permanent carers are a better choice, depending on how long the child has been in the care system. With the onset of adolescence we must consider the child's perception of what they need from the relationship. They may be aware of their birth family and have no wish for another mum and dad. They may purely be biding their time before they can choose where they will live and who they will live with when they are 16 years or over. If they need to be looked after in care then the long term or permanent care system may be considered.

Because of their life experience their placement has to be more tailored to fulfil as many of the young person's needs as possible. It would also have to take into consideration the length of time they would need the care. You can imagine that foster carers who wish to take on this responsibility are few and far between. They would remain carers rather than adopters simply to retain the support network of the Local Authority. Should these relationships blossom, and adolescent and carer both wish to formalise the arrangement then there is a mechanism in place to help them do that.

This is called a special guardianship. To all intents and purposes this has proven to be a very workable situation. It gives the child the benefit of having a stable relationship where positions are clearly defined but there is no conflict of title. For instance the young person can say on one side I have my mum and dad and on another side I have my guardian (foster carer), without feeling they are betraying anybody. When the young person reaches the age of 16 it will be anticipated that they would be looking towards leaving the Local Authority system.

The 16+ team

To help them through this time, there is a special team of social workers on hand known as the 16+ team. They will help guide them through their options. It is their job to look at every case in detail, assess how far down the road to independence the young person is and to help prepare them for the future.

These carers fulfil very varied roles. We know a carer who had a 15-year-old wayward boy, known to the police for minor infringements and cautions. The 16+ team were aware of him, and formed the opinion that the way he is leading his life is not the one he would choose. The carers decided to start by just being there for him and not passing judgment on his behaviour. They put very few boundaries in place for him, one of them being that by 9 pm he must have informed them of his intentions for that night. They attended the police station if they were called, again, not passing judgment, just being there for him. Gradually the boy began to respect his carers and understood that they were not trying to change his life, but they did care. He realised that the least he could do for them was to respond. Very slowly bonds were being built. When he finally became aware that the authority-allowed pocket money was not enough, the carer instigated in him the concept of a work ethic. The biggest hurdle the carer had to overcome was the boy's lack of self-esteem and the belief that he could not be of any use to anyone.

The carer noticed that when he was doing routine decorating around the home the boy showed interest and offered to help. They advised the 16+ team of this and in turn they sought a place for him in one of the trade development schemes. They suggested to the young man that it may be something he might like to consider and left it at that. A few weeks later after another altercation with the police, out of the blue he told the carer he would like to take up the offer of the course. Two years later he completed the course as a painter and decorator and was taken on by one of the big construction companies.

I have condensed this story but it is based on fact. Sadly there will be more failures than successes when you are dealing with this age group. If we can help 40% of these young people reach some of the potential that they themselves do not believe they have, then it is well worth trying.

19. Adoption Breakdown

Sadly adoptions do occasionally break down; there are no official records to refer to. There have been several surveys carried out, which would suggest that anything between 18% and 30% are classed as adoption breakdown. However the criteria used to measure these facts is somewhat patchy; they are by no way consistent. In my experience you are more likely to have problems when the adopted child reaches adolescence, and their true character is starting to evolve. They may choose to take different paths from what you expect or would choose for them. You should not feel that you have failed if this happens. Sometimes the consequences of their life before the adoption will begin to manifest its self. Adolescence can bring difficulties in ordinary family life, sometimes to the same extent.

You must treat these events as part of their character building process. Other influences may come into play; genetics will come to the foreground. We are only beginning to understand how important genetics are, and how big an influence they can have on our character and personality. A child's genetic build up can override everything. Even If a child has lived with you for 10 years and has enjoyed being part of your family for that time, those things may become difficult as they grow older, but it does not mean the adoption has failed.

This true story is an example of how an adoption could break down.

We fostered three East End children aged six, eight and ten, who were used to living a life a little on the rough side in a deprived area. They were placed for adoption with an architect, his wife and their 12-year-old son. These people were churchgoers and very much into scouting. They lived in a large detached house in the countryside. They were full of good intentions but the adoption broke down after only 11 months. The chasm between the children's previous life, and the new lifestyle with the adopters was too great for the children to adjust to.

This was many years ago and matching is far more intricate these days, but it is an example of what could happen. If there is one word that I could use to describe the contributing factor to many breakdowns it is "expectation" on behalf of the adopters and the children. It is wrong for adopters to expect that by giving a home to children it would be an immediate answer to all the children's problems. I am afraid that some adopters feel that by adopting the child within a few short months everything will be great. Then they have a vision of a happy contained family unit. It does not happen that way.

We have looked at how long it takes a foster child to adjust to a new family. It may take years, not months, for this to happen, and you as the adopter will just have to be patient. The same can be said about the child and their expectation of what they will achieve from adoption. They will feel that being a family may be all they wanted and expect to be fully integrated in to a family life in a very short time. They may find that living to your new rules and boundaries is a lot harder than they anticipated. Children will not immediately display gratitude and you should not expect it.

The following story is about one adoption that was alleged to have broken down. I know of an adoption of a three-year-old that over the years had all signs of working well. When the boy reached adolescence his whole perspective on his adoption changed. It became paramount for him to seek out his birth family. The adopters helped him with this and once he located his birth parents, he found it was not what he expected. They thought that as he had been adopted, he must have plenty of money and they wanted it, when this was not forthcoming they did not want to know him and told him to leave.

He became very angry at his disillusion and when he came home to the adopters, he was a different person. It was not long before he left his adopters' home with no notice; his adopters were devastated. They did not hear from him for 18 months and despite several attempts were unable to trace him. At this time the adopters thought the adoption had failed. However some time later he returned and was welcomed with open arms. He was very sorry for causing them so much upset and he has remained a full member of that family since. It seemed that he had just needed time to sort himself out.

It is with this case in mind that I question the criterion, which is used to gauge whether the adoption was successful. Whether the child is adopted or not, when they reach adolescence all kinds of extremes come into play, and do not always smooth out until this time in their life has passed.

Whilst some council`s provide post-adoption support this does not seem to be an ongoing situation. My advice to any adopter is not to leave it too long if you feel you or the child may need help in sorting things through. You may need to make yourself heard, but don't give up until you have your support. I feel many situations could be saved with a little professional intervention. You must not feel that asking for professional help is a reflection on your own abilities, even over the last three years if I felt I needed help I would ask for it.

20. Stories from the Light Side

So far I have been talking to you about the more serious situations that you may experience when fostering or adopting. To lighten things I would like to tell you some stories of the children that I fostered in the very early days of my fostering career. All details have been changed other than the event itself.

One Saturday lunchtime I received a telephone call from the emergency team who work out of normal hours, asking if I could take two children, a brother and sister aged six years and nine years. Their mother had gone into hospital to have another baby and after giving birth she had developed acute stomach pains. This had been diagnosed as appendicitis and had turned into peritonitis. In the meantime their father, who had been looking after the children, had collapsed with a suspected brain tumour. There was no family able to care for the children as they had moved to the East End of London from the north of England. The children were actually in the office with a suitcase of clothes and nowhere to go. I got their room ready and telephoned Roger to tell him to be prepared for two extras when he came home from work and that they would probably be very distressed.

The social workers arrived with these two beautifully dressed children. The boy was called George and his sister was Sally. He was a typical East End little boy and she was the prettiest little girl that you ever saw with beautiful long hair which shone and was perfectly groomed. They were more bewildered than distressed, but I showed them their room and we talked about how their mummy and daddy were not well and that they would be staying with me until mummy and daddy were much better.

So far so good, I got the tea ready, which they ate without comment and they were happy to play in the garden. I had explained that Roger would be home from work at around six and they were very keen to see him. As he walked up the path Sally and I opened the door to welcome him and at the same time George had found a tin tray and proceeded to the top of the stairs.

"Hello I am Sally", she blurted out to Roger.

At the same time, George came down the stairs sliding on the tray whilst saying "Hello mate and I am George". Clearly Roger was prepared for distressed, what he was greeted with was anything but.

I got them ready for bed while Roger had his dinner and it was clear they were not yet tired and so Roger said they could watch Tarzan on the television with him.

"Have you ever been in the jungle?" George asked Roger.

"Oh yes many times," was the reply (news to me, I thought).

"Have you ever swung from tree to tree like that?"

"Yes often," replied Roger.

"Have you ever fought a lion?"

"Once or twice," came the reply.

"Cooooor," said George. The next morning after breakfast George asked to play in the field. "What field?" I asked.

"The one out the back," George replied. The penny dropped, he meant our back garden. When Sally and I were talking I learnt that they lived in a high rise flat, and for George your own field was a thing to be cherished.

On the next Monday at 2 pm the social workers came to take them to see their mum and dad in the hospital. When they returned they were both physically and emotionally worn out. They had their tea then got ready for bed and just about stayed awake to see Roger come home.

In the evening I received a lovely phone call from their mum and we chatted for ages and I was able to get valuable information with regard to the children's likes and dislikes etc.

In all they stayed for around six weeks. On the Friday afternoon I received a call to say that both mum, dad and baby were to be discharged on the following Monday morning and the parents would like to come and pick the children up. News that thrilled the children to bits, but Sally assured me that she would really miss me. It was very clear that the only thing George was going to miss was the "field" out the back.

To break the tension of waiting for Monday we decided that on the Saturday we would take the children to the zoo, on the train. Off we set, George barely able to contain his excitement. "Haven't you been to the zoo before?" Roger asked.

"Oh yes", came their joint reply.

We arrived and George was keen to take Roger's hand and drag him from exhibit to exhibit until he had finally got Roger to the front of the lion's cage. Obviously this is a very crowded location. Then in his loudest voice he said, "Go on then Roger, you said you could fight lions, get in there and fight that one". I could see Roger was trying to keep him placated but George was having none of it and by now the surrounding crowd had cottoned on and were laughing and some men were saying "yeah go on Roger fight that one". I decided to end Roger's embarrassment and tempt George away with the suggestion of candy floss.

The children were collected by their very grateful parents on the Monday and for several years we received Christmas cards with photos and there was always a drawing of a lion from George.

As time passed I learnt that you cannot win them all when it comes to children in care, but enjoying the good experiences makes the other ones easier to bear.

Our home at that time was a small terraced house with postage stamp back garden. To us it was nothing out of the ordinary. To George and Sally it was a field where they played happily for hours having great adventures. This lesson in appreciating what you have was repeated many times and Roger and I learnt that children have long memories and take what you say quite literally.

A few years later Roger and I purchased a rather large Victorian semi-detached house built in 1901. It had four bedrooms, three reception rooms and a large kitchen/diner. It was in poor condition when we bought it but we quickly decorated and made it presentable. I had my own two girls at this time and despite having one or two young foster children we were fairly rattling around in it.

As a foster carer you are prone to having random spot visits from Social Services and one day I had a visit from the head of fostering and adoption. After her inspection we were having a cup of tea and discussing children coming into care in general. She explained that they had no difficulty in placing one child and at a push could keep two together, but when three or four siblings came into care there was no alternative than to split the children up. From the children's point of view this made a bad situation much worse. It is hard for children to settle normally, and the addition of being split from their siblings must be very hard on them.

With the extra space we had, she wondered if I would consider turning two of the unused rooms into bedrooms to take three to four children in each large room, specifically to keep sibling groups together. I would have up to six foster children placed with me. She would supply the bunk beds and furnishings and I would have a cleaner and a cook to help. I could select whom I wished but she would have to vet them and interview them as well. I agreed to give it a try and after three months and several safety checks later we were up and running. She went onto explain that this was her own initiative and she would have to take full responsibility for us as well as the children and therefore she would have to have unfettered access to our home at all times.

We did not realise to what extent her visits would make, as she would call before breakfast and as late as 8 pm at night. All of this was unannounced. She was a very tall lady and would enter with very few words and a clipboard. Then she would go through the property top to bottom. It wasn't till this ritual had finished that she would relax.

One of the first calls to take advantage of this accommodation was three little boys who had been taken into emergency care. I won't go into details as to why they had come into care other than to say they had been living in a halfway house with their parents. The boys aged three, four and eight were at a London hospital where they had just had all their hair shaved off because they had ringworm. This is a scalp condition of the fungi type and is highly contagious. I agreed to take them and was told a consultant from the hospital would ring me with advice on how to manage their condition. The consultant phoned and explained that the boys would need to wear skull caps at all times for a few weeks. They would have to have fresh caps daily and the old ones were to be burnt. There were ointments to use and all of my family would have to be checked weekly for any signs of the infection.

The boys arrived and they looked so sad and dishevelled, their clothes were filthy and so were they. I took them straight upstairs for a bath and left Roger to sort out an old suitcase tied with string containing their clothes. When I came down with the boys wrapped in towels, Roger had the clothes in the washing machine on a hot wash. Some of their clothes fitted where they touched but I managed to top them up with spares that I had accumulated.

The boys settled down, and I managed to get the eldest boy, let's call him Alex, into school and he was really picking up well. They were having fortnightly visits home, this was going well and their parents were beginning to get to grips with their problems.

It was after one of these visits that the boys had come back tired but happy. They had their tea and a bath and I had put the two youngest to bed leaving Alex up for a while, as he was a good bit older. After an hour or so I was tucking him up in bed when he said he had enjoyed his visit but was glad to be back.

"That's nice," I said. "What do you like most about being here?"

"Guess," he replied.

"Television, school, food," said I.

"No, "he said.

"I give up," I finally said.

He snuggled down in bed, pulled up the bedclothes and said, "Clean sheets". Of all the things he could have said, the thing that he appreciated the most was probably the simplest thing that I could have provided. I have never forgotten this and sometimes wonder if we complicate things a little too much instead of focusing on the basics.

In these little anecdotes I have changed many of the details but not the facts. In this instance the boys' parents got themselves completely sorted out and the boys were able to return home in stages and finally leaving my care after 13 months. As far as I am aware they never went into care again.

One thing that has been consistent over the years is that there is always a duty social worker on call day and night all the year through. One of the first children to come into care with me was by a call from a duty social worker at 11.45 one night after a call from the police. They had found a two-year-old little girl wandering around the streets of London in her nightwear and carrying a baby's bottle half-full of cold tea.

Enquiries had revealed nothing and the police needed a place for her for one night at least. I agreed to take her and within half an hour she was with us bottle and all. What was remarkable about this little girl was that other than being a little grubby she did not appear to be fazed by the whole event. I gave her a wash and put her to bed and she was asleep in a very short time. In the morning I received a telephone call from Social Services to say that the little girl's name was Letty.

Letty's mother had left her with a neighbour for the night. The neighbour had put her to bed in a downstairs room and then gone to bed herself. Letty must have woken up and literally gone walkabout without anybody knowing. I was advised that Letty was to stay with me for a few days while the whole situation was investigated.

At this time my own little girl was the same age as Letty and I managed to sort her out some clothes. In a very short time the two girls became quite good friends. So much so that I had taken a few photographs of them, sitting on the settee and playing in the garden.

After about ten days, Letty's mum and a social worker came and collected her and she went off home.

When I look back on those days I cannot help but feel how relaxed things were with children coming into care. If there was any concern, the child came into care until things were sorted out and then quite usually they went home

One day I received a call to ask if I could take three siblings into my care, two boys aged nine and ten and their little sister aged seven. I was only given their surname.

The children arrived and were in a very distressed state, all three of them. I cannot recall the exact circumstances under which they came into care. I made a fuss of them as usual and when I had a close look at the little girl I thought, I know that face. Yes it was Letty but not the laid back Letty that I had known four years ago. She was gaunt, distressed and frightened.

After a while I managed to get them settled down and then I remembered the photo album. We all sat down on the floor. "I have something to show you," I said. I was able to show them the photographs of Letty when she had been with me before.

As the penny dropped she shouted, "That's me!" It was amazing to see how her little face changed and it was obvious that she was beginning to remember. Her becoming more at ease began to rub off on her brothers and when my own little girl came home from school there was plenty of excitement especially from the two girls.

They stayed with us for about 18 months and then they went on to be adopted all together by a lovely couple, whose family had all grown up. Sad to say I never knew how things turned out, there were no cards or photos sent. As I have said before we were not privy to their address in those long ago days.

With a family group home I had to adapt to children coming at short notice and on some occasions for a very short period of time. It seemed I was always changing beds. On one occasion I was asked to take a six-year-old boy whose father was in prison and had a few months left of his sentence. His mother had gone missing. The little boy had been living with his grandmother who, tragically and unexpectedly, had passed away. He was placed with me as an emergency until a more suitable long-term placement could be found.

He stood out from the other children I had with me at the time as he had plenty of clothes and was already used to a routine. It was clear his grandmother had been doing a very good job.

He had to share a bedroom with two younger boys and it soon became apparent that he had not been used to living with other children however, he appeared to settle down very well.

On reflection I felt perhaps a little too well. A week or so passed and things were still progressing nicely when I began to smell a rather peculiar smell in the three boys' bedroom. It was an odd smell not easily identifiable. I cleaned the room thoroughly checking the drawers, washing the bedding and all the time I could not find anything that contained this peculiar smell. After a further few days the smell had increased to such a degree that Roger had to strip the room right out. He emptied the wardrobes taking all the clothes out and putting them in another room. Then the bedding and the mattresses followed. He began to take out the drawers that went under the bed then he stopped. "It's here," he said. Behind the drawer under the little boy's bed he found several small cylindrical parcels about two to three inches long and an inch wide. Some were wrapped in tissues and some in silver foil. Upon opening them we found them to contain dried poo.

I have to admit that at first I was horrified, but then I felt very sad and wondered why it had happened. What did this mean? At the time I had a very good doctor who was young and recently qualified. I telephoned the surgery and told them what had happened. Within 20 minutes I had a call from a psychiatrist who was based at Kings College Hospital in London. He sounded a lovely man. I was told to ask Roger to get some stone or wood and wrap them in tissues and silver paper to look just the same as the parcels we had found. We were to put these back where we had found the others. Then put everything back the way it was and say nothing to anyone especially the little boy concerned.

When I asked him what did all this mean he said, "It's quite simple really, this little lad has lost his dad, then his mum and now he has lost his grandmother. It is not surprising that he feels he has nothing of his own at all. Nothing that is, except his own poo. Something of his own, something tangible and because it has come from his own body, it is his very own in every sense of the word".

He went on to say that we must make a point of telling all the children how important it is to wash their hands after using the toilet and keep re-affirming this on a daily basis. We were also to wait for a convenient time when the boys were out of the room, remove and replace any new parcels on a daily basis. He also told how our doctor had been a student of his and he was going to ring him and advise how he should treat this little boy with counselling.

It was marvellous to see that after a while, with counselling, the parcel delivery service came to an end.

The lesson I learned from my experience with this little man was that when I was feeling a little hard done by I should not to feel too sorry for myself for nothing could compare with how lonely and lost he must have felt.

After a few months social workers contacted us to say that the little man's father was being released from prison and wanted to be reunited with his son. I am pleased to say that he eventually returned to live with his father.

Running the family group home meant that besides the children, there was a constant flow of social workers, health visitors and assorted others that would all be making visits. Fitting round these visits proved to be a task of its own and this meant that organising any days out was especially difficult. However one summer's day Roger had managed to secure the loan of a minibus from a friend. My cook/man Friday (who was also a good friend and a lady), my cleaner and her five-year-old son, six foster children, our two girls, Roger and I all set off for a day at the seaside. Complete with pack up lunches, bottles of pop and an assortment of buckets and spades. The excitement was at fever pitch.

None of the six foster children had ever been to the seaside before but that did not stop their talk of swimming in the sea, diving of off rocks, and building humungous sandcastles. One young man was especially excited; he bore the nickname Black Jack which was given to him by the other children and had nothing to do with his skin tone. It was more to do with the fact that he used to love four-for-a-penny Black Jack liquorice sweets, to such an extent that the other children would get Black Jack doing errands for the reward of a black jack sweet.

I do not know if you are aware of the north Kent coast but it is not exactly known for its sandy beaches; more varying grades of shingle fit the bill. Around noon we arrived, disembarked and laid towels in the form of a semi-circle and backed this with windbreakers to form our own little enclosure. We had devised a rota system of counting bodies every 15 minutes just to make sure that we did not lose anybody. The beach was busy with families. As we unpacked we came to realise that these children did not know what the seaside was. We pointed to the large expanse of water explaining that was the sea. We pointed out ships and other explanations. Black Jack stood there at the water's edge entranced and totally speechless. The waves were splashing over his sandals, and with an unopened black jack sweet in his hand he said, "Where's the sea?"

It was a lovely day, the children joined in with other children playing beach games. We counted them all back into the bus and started for home. We had just got to the top of the beach road when Roger stopped the bus. When I asked what the matter was he said, "I have just seen a face in the mirror and it's not one of ours". On recounting, we had the right number but one was a stowaway. We quickly turned round and returned to the beach expecting to find scenes of panic. What we did find was our missing one, playing sand castles with other children, and holding an ice cream. The family of the stowaway had not realised that their child was missing; they were using the same method of head count as us. We travelled home all singing. Gradually there were less singing, as they were all fast asleep.

I had the family group home for about four years and had to close when the manager who instigated the concept left Social Services to go to work for a charitable organisation. At this time Social Services were being reconstructed and no one would take the responsibility for us. We reverted back to normal sized foster carers taking up to three children at a time. But I was very sorry to see it end as it had been a lot of fun, with lots of good memories.

21. Letters from Other Adopters

As I have previously stated the whole concept of this book was at the behest of some of the adopters I have had the pleasure and honour of working with. Whilst writing I asked many of them if they would like to contribute a note or letter to state how adoption has worked for them. Here are a few of their contributions.

From J and S

The support and understanding that Jacqueline and Roger had for us has been immeasurable in its benefit to us, we cannot thank them enough.

From P and L

We were asked to put a few words in the book. We are so grateful to all the people involved with our adoption. Our son is a delight he has changed our lives and is now at school. Thank you so much for all the help and advice that we received.

From P and S

Roger asked us if we would like to contribute a few lines to your book as to how adopting two children changed our life. It was a simple request, hard to do, because our life has changed so much. We went from being a working couple without children, on what seemed to be an endless waiting list, for a year or more. Then in a period of six weeks we were a family of four. We look back to that time and remember how daunting it all seemed. Now we are a complete family and our lives are so content. We cannot bear the thought of being without our two wonderful children. The way it is going it may not be too long before we are Grandparents. Only jok ing our son is such a one for the girls at this minute. Our daughter is all squirrels and hedgehogs a proper little conservationist she is. So in a nutshell adoption has given us everything.

Our experience of adoption by Colette & John

Where do you start … When we finally decided that adoption was the route to us having a family, we began our journey along the long road. The thought of no children for us was not an option, we had tried everything else and we were certain we wanted to embark on this life-changing journey. We felt we had so much to give and we wanted to give it all. Then had a couple of meetings with our local social services office who were very helpful, this resulted with us attending a one week course where we could learn lots more about the process and ourselves.

At the end of this course we felt stronger than ever, this was our destiny. We had a further meeting with our social worker and agreed that we would get ourselves approved to adopt three children. Three I hear you say! Well that's one hell of a commitment. Well they say ignorance is bliss, and when we had family stay with us who have a child we realised that this may indeed be a little ambitious. We decided therefore to change our application to potential approval for two children. Our thoughts were of wanting our family all in one go which would be less upheaval for both us and our future children going through multiple single adoptions.

The approval process was both tough and highly intrusive, but we understand absolutely necessary. We had weekly visits from our social worker as we unravelled our relationship checked in all the nooks and crannies and then put it all back together. At the end of the process, which took the best part of a year, our case was put before a panel for approval. This is one of the many milestones of this process and a milestone we managed to pass without issue.

Then we entered the quiet period, going from all that activity to a waiting game. Will it be a week and month, a year or more? Who knows but this is the difficult period for all approved adopters, the not knowing, waiting for the phone call. Your life hanging in the balance knowing out there somewhere are your children waiting for a connection to be made.

We are one of the lucky ones; the wait was just a couple of weeks. We were working from home when the phone rang…. It was our social worker with some news! "Would you be interested in three little girls?" Yes Yes…. was our answer to all three. They were aged 2, 3 and 4 and currently living together in foster care. But hold on we are only approved for two children, how will this work. We learned that the panel can reconvene and uplift our approval from two to three children. This was quickly arranged and we were duly approved to adopt three children.

Now this is where things happen at a pace, a fast pace. We were desperate to learn more, lots more. Every scrap of information was a golden nugget, photos are not allowed at this stage. It was felt that we need to fully understand about these three little girls before the images were burned into our heads, potentially clouding our judgment in some way. When files were available the local office offered to post them, no we said as we jumped into the car to collect them immediately in person. We read every word several times and we were convinced that these were our girls and a perfect match had been made.

The next stage was a meeting with the social workers of the girls. The girls lived in a different part of the country and therefore we had to meet the approval of the social services local to them who had been managing their case. The meeting was set to happen at our house and was to be attended by three social workers, our own and the two from the girls' side. This meeting went well and lots of questions were asked and our home was briefly inspected for suitability. We noticed on the table a brown envelope marked photos… this was a distraction I have to say. At the end of the meeting all must have been well as we were asked if we would like to see a picture of the girls. This was the first time we saw our three beautiful daughters, I can't lie there were a few tears.

What next? Well we would meet the girls at the foster carers home the following week, at this point is was only two weeks since the first phone call… like I said things were happening fast. There was an introduction plan put in place, we were to spend a full week with them at the foster carers, and this would be followed by a full week spent with us at our house. They would not be staying overnight but boarded at a local B&B. At the foster carers it would start with just an hour on the first day, followed by a little longer the next, building up to visits to the park etc. It was also arranged to vary the times of the visits so we could see the morning, afternoon and evening routines. The plan would be duplicated at our house but like I say at night they would go back to the B&B.

Well the day soon came and we were staying in hotel not too far from the house of the foster carers, we didn't sleep too much that night. We had arranged to meet them at 11 am and the morning dragged, eventually we got in the car full for nervous excitement. The children were prepared for the visit as we had made of an album with our pictures along with pictures of their soon to be home. We pulled up on the road outside the home of the foster carers Jacqui & Roger, got out of the car and walked down the path of the immaculate bungalow to be greeted at the door by Roger. As we stood on the step we could hear the sound of girls giggling, our hearts pounding as we were invited in and made our way down the hall into the lounge.

There they were our three little angels, the youngest clinging to Jacqui in a bear hug peaking at us with a big cheeky smile. The other two were playing, they said hello and invited us to play in their games. The enormity of the responsibility hit us like a steam train along with an instant bond and it was a huge privilege to be called mummy Colette and daddy John on the first day. Jacqui and Roger were so lovely; it was obvious that they loved the wonderful work they do. We spent two unforgettable hours with our girls. They gave us a tour of the house and showed us their toys. The time soon came to go and we had to say goodbye until the next day.

Next morning soon arrived, and we felt much more relaxed this time and so looking forward to seeing the girls. We arrived and again Roger opened the door, the girls came straight to us and were obviously also more relaxed. They dropped our first names and just called us mummy and daddy, this was a big thing for us and everything was starting to feel very real. We played, had a cup of tea and it was decided a trip to the park was in order. We had a great time and we did take a little video footage, the girls with their cute cockney accents loved to play and pretend that there were tigers in the trees. We tired them out and headed back. The week was full of activity and with each *day that passed, we all relaxed and the bonds grew stronger and stronger.*

At the end of the week we said our goodbyes and headed back on the long journey home, head spinning and smiles beaming. It was our turn now to be the hosts and we planned our week of activities for the coming week. We entered this new world of parents planning trips to parks and play centres, planning meals, things that are now part of our normal life. I have to admit, our house was immaculate, not a thing out of place, the lawn neatly trimmed, the car gleaming inside and out … boy how things have changed.

The girls arrived at our house and were a little shy at first, understandable with new surroundings and a strange place. They soon relaxed and explored the house; they would each have their very own room. The week flew by and we noticed that Jacqui and Roger very carefully drifting into the background and let us take the reins. We could see this must have been very difficult for them after caring for the girls for 12 months, but they handled it most professionally in front of us and the girls. Again the week flew by and the girls were to travel back to Jacqui and Rogers for the last time spend the night there. All their belongings were to be packed up and we would collect them this time for good.

We drove back this time no social worker, child seats firmly fixed to the back seat, this was it. We arrived at Jacqui and Rogers and it was not difficult to see the emotion in their eyes, how do they do this, its takes a very special person indeed to do their job so well. The three suitcases sat in the hall, I picked them up and Roger helped me load the car, he was holding it together… just. They gave hugs and kisses and the best thing was to be quick as it would be best for everyone. We securely fastened the girls into the new shiny car seats and we climbed in the front ready to set off. We looked around to see three smiley faces, started the engine and waved goodbye. I can only imagine how difficult it must have been for Jacqui and Roger as they waved us off. I know they made plans that day to keep themselves busy as this was their way of getting through the first day.

Three hours driving and a few toilet stops later we arrived home, the girls ran into the now familiar house as we unpacked the car, we had made it. I will never forget that first night, we bathed the girls, put on their pj's, and read bedtime stories. They were soon asleep after the long day. We kept checking on them making sure they were settled, pinching ourselves, yesterday there were two of us now there were five.

We are writing this over eight years later and shortly after adopting the girls we defied science to become pregnant and we now also have a little boy. The girls love him so much and he them. We will be eternally grateful to the wonderful work done by Jacqui and Roger in preparing the girls so well to move on. They get children in the raw state, after suffering let's face it bad things. They give them stability and love all the time knowing they will one day let them move on to their new lives.

From Dee Dee

We adopted our son when he was five. From the moment he walked in he was a real presence in our house. He came with some fear and anxiety, a desire to be in control, hyper-vigilance, a busy nature and constant chatter! But, he also arrived with a default cheerfulness, a desire to please, an openness to love and be loved, an incredible resilience and a natural charm.

The first night he spent in our house, my husband, myself and our 7-year-old son, were all quite nervous and anxious. We were so aware of how scary it must have been for him, a five-year-old, to suddenly be living with people he barely knew. We watched Fireman Sam, read stories, and settled him in bed with the big yellow stuffed duck he brought with him. I clearly remember the sense of peace and contentment I felt when both boys were asleep in bed that night. After years of unsuccessfully trying to have another child, and then years of going through the adoption process, our family was finally complete.

Now most of our days are filled with busyness in the way that most families are, but every now and then we stop and have a proper look and realise what a long way he and we have come. Recently, he went away for two nights on a school trip. After five years it was just the three of us again. The first night he was away we enjoyed the chance to cherish our older son. We took him out to dinner, let him stay up a bit late and enjoyed the chance to focus completely on him. But, the next morning, the house felt very quiet and very empty. We missed our chatty little boy very much.

What have we learned in these past five years?

Just because our son smiles all the time and is always cheerful, does not mean that he is fine. He smiles as a coping mechanism when he is anxious. When he is in trouble he will often smile all the more, which can get him in more trouble if an adult is expecting contrition! Look beyond the smile.

For us, setting limits has been key. We have had to work hard at this because sometimes it can feel a bit tough. But, he definitely feels safer and more secure with clear limits.

Having 'special time' with our older son was essential in the first few years. He had had 7 years of being an only child. It was a real shock to suddenly have to share us – especially and to share us with someone who wanted our full attention all the time. He was able to stay up an hour later every night and have time alone with us. We also spend time each weekend with each boy individually.

For us, and for others we have spoken to, managing schools has been a challenge. We have had to been very involved in school to ensure our son's needs are met and that he feels safe. We know now, never to assume teachers will understand the needs of a child with attachment issues. We start each year getting to know each new teacher and helping the teacher to understand our son.

And, we have learned so much about ourselves – our limits, our strengths, our weaknesses.

It's not been an easy five years but we have loved being a family, together, the four of us. We have made loads of mistakes and definitely have wished we could have parented better at times. But, somehow we have muddled through. We know we are lucky to have two lovely boys who challenge us most days but also love us and bring us so much joy.

From Claire

We finally met our beautiful baby S in December 2012. It had been an anxious time for us as birth dad had made occasional contact with Social Workers but had never followed through with anything concrete. His latest contact was the afternoon prior to us seeing her for the first time. There was a moment of complete panic for us when a Social Worker who was not really involved in our case, said we might have to *postpone meeting her. Luckily for us permission was granted for intro`s to begin as planned. We went to bed nervously excited about the next day.*

I will always remember Roger opening the door in his larger than life voice welcoming us into his home and introducing Jacqueline with S. She was so small wearing a little cream knitted top with grey tights. Her hair was short and she had a chubby little face. She was happy and content and you could see how much love Roger and Jacqueline had for her. It shone out of them and love radiated from baby S. She was such a happy little person and remains this way to this day. She is very rarely upset and rarely only cries if she is actually in pain. I think that the loving, stable and kind start that she had with her foster mu m and dad allowed her to trust people and to attach to us really well and quickly. She had confidence! Even at that young age of 10 months and this improves the older she gets.

Our Initial visit went well and Roger and Jacqueline allowed us a little time quietly doing things in the kitchen or bedroom but always popping in and out of the lounge so that S felt secure. Everything they did was done to benefit baby S and her transition into our family.

It must have been incredibly hard to see at times as every day was a day closer to her leaving them. Although they obviously were happy for her they must have felt very sad at times. This was kept to themselves which made things very much easier for us and S.

From the moment we walked into their beautiful home they began the slow process of distancing themselves from S and encouraging her to look to us for food, nappy change, comfort etc. They were still there for her with a smile or encouraging word, but they did not pick her up too much or make too much fuss. This allowed baby S a bit of freedom to get to know us.

The second day we returned in the morning and I think I gave her breakfast. We had a lovely morning and again lots of encouragement for S to look to us rather than Jacqueline for comfort or milk etc. Jacqueline was always popping in and out of the room (no Fuss). This gave S that little bit of security which she was looking for.

We introduced our son Dexter and Aunty Betty and again just spent time getting to know each other and playing with toys etc. It all went well. The reassurances offered by Jacqueline and Rogers presence really did give S lots of confidence and by this time we were getting along quite well. Jacqueline throughout all this time quietly told us all about baby S and what she liked/ did not like, things that she had done etc. We got to know her routine and stuck by it.

We progressed to a little walk to the post office and I remember S crying so we came home.

We arrived into her life just a she began teething and the teething carried on for the next 8 months or so (lucky us). Our final Hurdle was a trip out on our own with S to Blue Water (Kent).

I will always have fond memories of this massive shopping mall because it was the first place we ever took her to. We ate in John Lewis and sat listening to carol singers for ages, before spending "hours" in Waterstones our son Dexter is book mad. It was a lovely day and by this time baby S was getting used to us.

Our last morning in Kent was spent chatting to the Social Worker and being monitored by her in Jacqueline and Rogers's home. It all went fine and we headed off to catch a flight back to where we live in Scotland. Jacqueline Roger and baby S started their long drive up to Scotland in their car.

Roger and Jacqueline stayed in a lovely little holiday let in our home village. Each day they would drop S at ours and spend less and less time with us before heading out for a few hours.

Towards the end of the intro`s birth dad again made contact by writing a letter saying he wanted S. We were contacted by our Social Worker to say that things might have to be delayed and we would not be able to have her come to live with us until it was somehow resolved. I had a complete meltdown as by this time we had grown so attached to her The thought of her not being ours was frightening, also it would have destroyed our son as he loved S from the moment he met her and she adores him. Her first word every morning is where is Dexter. They really do love each other.

We were in Mother Care when the call came through and we went straight back to Jacqueline and Rogers to drop her off. We were very worried. As soon as we walked in Roger gave us a big hug and tried to ease our worries. He talked about how these things can happen and that it is usually just a last minute panic on behalf of the parent but they do not usually follow through.

It turned out to be true here as S`s birth dad did not do anything legally required to keep her the decision was made that her best interests would be met by staying with us. Huge relief but Jacqueline and Rogers pep talk helped us to remain calm.

We collected S (quickly) from them the next day and took her home to spend life with Mummy Daddy Dexter and Molly and Misty our cats. Bliss. We all love her very much and cannot imagine life without her. She is the happiest, loveliest, funniest child ever it has been wonderful.

We keep in contact with Jacqueline and Roger and they plan to visit us in Scotland this year and hopefully next year. I really feel it is best for S to know the wonderful foster parents who looked after and loved first. They named her and we actually gave her a middle name of Jacqueline. It is important for S given the circumstances to know she was loved from birth and that they will still know each other in the years to come. Jacqueline and Roger are wonderful people. Thank you for S xxxxx

From Jenny

It took almost 4 years from our initial phone call to our Local Authority to the day that we met our son.

We met our son for the first time at the home of his foster carers with whom he had been placed since he was only a few months old. At the time of introduction he was 3years and 8 months old. They were the only family he could remember. The pain of him moving was profound. It is not easy to try to explain to a 3 year old why he has to move from a home in which he was settled and where people loved him. He was quite clear (when he realised that he was not with us for an extended holiday) that he did not want a forever mummy and daddy, he did not want to stay with us and definitely wanted to go back,

Over time this has diminished to the point now where we feel he is, on the whole, settled.

Meet ups with his foster carers are happy occasions and he looks forward to seeing them. We feel that it is a positive experience for all involved. If, like us, you have contact with foster carers *please try not to feel threatened or that your position as your child`s mummy and daddy is compromised. Contact is not for you or the foster carers (although we all like seeing each other) but for your child to help them make sense of their life and circumstances in which they came to be adopted by you. At first, it may be difficult and undoubtedly you will see some fall out in terms of behaviour after these events, but I would urge you to persevere unless there are strong and compelling reasons not to do so.*

In writing this, we thought about what we might have liked to know when we were placed with a child or indeed the matching process.

Firstly, you do not have to say "yes" to the first child that is placed in front of you. It is hard but try to remain detached. Can you raise this child to adulthood and beyond? What are the red flags from the paperwork that you have been given? You are not shopping for a child, but you should be as near to certain as you can be that you can cope with whatever this child may throw at you. Quite possibly the child that you read about on paper will be nothing like the child that you end up with. Do not be pressurised by social workers who, at times, can seem like double gazing salesmen when they are talking to you about a child they are trying to place. They need you. If you have been approved you are deemed suitable to adopt. Take your time. Your child is out there.

Secondly it seems obvious but adoption is about finding families for children and not to fill a gap for a child in your familyhowever you have come to adoption. Your child probably will not say "Thank you for adopting me!" indeed, they should not feel that they should be grateful to you. They are not lucky to have been adopted. They are simply able, by adoption, to have what they should have had from the beginning. It is every child`s right to have a loving and stable family. Adoption is a good solution to the less than ideal circumstances in which our children found themselves through no fault of their own.

Thirdly, it is OK to regret your decision to adopt and wonder why the hell you ever agreed to this whirling mass of distraction entering your home and lives. At times, the behaviour of our adopted child has been awful. In our darkest times we could not believe that we had voluntarily signed up to this chaos. Try to keep going, in the vast majority of cases it does get better. It is OK not to love your adopted child at first and it is also OK, at times, not to like them. Forming relationships with strangers takes time, Sometimes, a long time.

Now, we love our adopted son as we love our birth children. This did not happen overnight. Do not feel bad about this. There is nothing to be gained from chastising yourself and drowning in guilt or feelings of inadequacy. Your adopted child needs you to be there for them. If you cannot regulate your own feelings then there is little hope that they will be able to make sense of the fear and terror that they are feeling.

Lastly, we feel it very important to be honest about our child`s adoption and the circumstances that led to him being removed from his birth family and being placed with us. This is not the same thing as being negative about his birth family .No good can come of running down your child`s birth family or hiding them away. They are part of your child and have contributed to making him or her, the amazing person that they are today. You are not your child`s first mummy or daddy. They have and will always have a birth mother and father. This should be acknowledged. Do not make them feel that it is a choice or competition between you. They are entitled to have both valued within their lives. They deserve to be given the space to explore this and to know that you are in charge of your feelings surrounding this difficult area. Your child will not care whether you feel uncomfortable about or angry with their birth parents but will quickly pick up on whether this is an area that is off limits. We did not want our child to feel that his past was shameful. We wanted to convey the message that-yes-the care he received was poor in his birth family but that is not the same as his birth mother being a bad person. I consider that our child has 2 mothers, the mother that gave birth to him and me, the mother who gets to raise him. I fully expect that he will want to meet with her and we will be fully supportive of whatever decision he chooses to make regarding this in the future.

Whatever you think, the birth family are not going anywhere and if you tuck them away in a dark corner only to be brought out on High days and holidays you are creating a ghost that will come back to haunt you. Just because you are not talking about them does not mean that your child is not thinking about them. Talk about it and it will help take the sting out of the tail of a potential explosive situation.

Keep in mind that adoption is not a roses around the door, skip off into the sunset happy ending. Lower your expectations to virtually nil. Prepare for the worst and hope for the best and you may be pleasantly surprised. To us, adoption has been a joy. We feel very fortunate that we get to be parents to a lively, affectionate and kind little boy. To be able to see a child blossom and be part of their life is an incredible gift and we do not take the responsibility lightly.

22. A Final Word

I hope that as you have come this far, I have been able to give you a reasonable insight into how the adoption process works. It may not be the best system in the world but I can assure you that most of the people involved work hard to improve it month by month. In these times of austerity nowhere do cuts to budgets implode more than in children's services. I feel that if politicians were to stop looking at children's services as expenditure and instead look upon them as an investment for the future perhaps we could achieve more.

Fostering and adoption has been a major part of my life, when I sit back I can reflect on the many children whose lives I have been a very small part of. I feel privileged to have cared for these children and although this time had its ups and downs I would not have changed anything. You cannot win them all but that is the nature of being human. I hope you find the strength and will to proceed and please be assured you will make a difference to at least one little soul.